Isabel Ryrie
Oxford - March 1991.

Mystics
For Our
Time

Mystics
For Our
Time

Carmelite Meditations
for a New Age

Noel O' Donoghue

T&T CLARK
EDINBURGH

T&T CLARK LTD
59 GEORGE STREET
EDINBURGH EH2 2LQ
SCOTLAND

First Published 1989

ISBN 0 567 09526 6

British Library Cataloguing in Publication Data
O' Donoghue, Noel
Mystics for our time.
1. Christian life. Mysticism. Biographies.
Collections
I. Title
248.2'2'0922

Typeset by Buccleuch Printers Ltd, Hawick
Printed and Bound in Great Britain by Billing & Sons Ltd, Worcester

This book is dedicated with love and admiration to my sisters and brothers in the Order of the Blessed Virgin Mary of Mount Carmel.

NOEL DERMOT O'DONOGHUE, ODC

CONTENTS

Part III
Cloister and Cosmos: St Thérèse of Lisieux

INTRODUCTION

This book is the fruit of a life-long meditation – philosophical, theological, mystical and, above all, personal. Personal in the sense that it is the story of personal encounters in the high places of the heart and mind. In her own time and place many of those who met Teresa of Jesus (whom we know as St Teresa of Avila) were marked for life by the encounter, as in our own day was Edith Stein, the brilliant Jewish pupil of Edmund Husserl, the father of modern philosophy. So, too, in his own day and in our day, the voice of John of the Cross, poet of the sacred marriage of the human soul with that eternal beauty whence it comes, has called those who could hear it to that austerest of journeys, to that mountain-top of enduring peace and substantial joy. But it is, above all, Thérèse of Lisieux and her mystical 'atheism' that speaks to the depths of our unbelieving and despairing hearts in this century of darker 'Satanic mills' than even Blake could have imagined.

I want to share my friends with my friends, my people with my people: this above all is the reason for writing and publishing these meditations. Old friends and new friends: the Carmelite way is a way of friendship; the Carmelite vision opens to that light above the mind which St Augustine discovered in Plotinus, the Platonist, before he could see it in the New Testament. This, Augustine tells us, is the light that charity knows: the light of understanding that is also the fire in the heart. These great Carmelite

mystics are people of light and fire: they are my people,
and I want to share them with whoever has glimpses of the
light and feels the kindling of the fire. We belong together
in the Carmelite way, and we share the ancient vision of the
hermits of Mount Carmel, whether or not we become
members of the first, second or third Order of Our Lady of
Mount Carmel. In a concluding chapter I have looked at
the Carmelite vision in its origins and its contribution to
our understanding of the community of men and women
today.

The immediate occasion for writing down these meditations was an invitation from Fr. Cronan Glynn ODC,
Prior of the Oxford Priory of Discalced Carmelites. The
chapter on 'The Four Spirits' resulted from a visit to the
Carmelite sisters at Presteigne, Powys, Wales, where I
spent a week striving to unravel a problem in the *Dark
Night of the Soul* of St John of the Cross. Light came, at
least partial light, but, as in all the other meditations, it is
love that truly illuminates, not the easy and comfortable
love that condones and connives, but that piercing love that
searches the heart for the truth in oneself and in the other:
the Sword of Elijah that dominates the Carmelite coat of
arms whose motto is *Zelo zelatus sum pro domino Deo
exercituum* (I am on fire with love for the God of all the
heavenly host). These words go back to Elijah himself, the
man of fire who nevertheless knew times of discourage-
ment and depression. But he held to his Carmel vision, all
the way.

This work was conceived as a unit, but it incorporates a
talk on St Teresa given at Trinity and All Souls College,
Leeds, in 1981, and published as a chapter of *St Teresa de
Jésus and Her World* edited by Margaret A. Rees (Leeds,
1981). The section on St John of the Cross forms Vol. 27 of
The Living Flame series published by the Carmelite Centre

of Spirituality (Dublin, 1984). I am happy to acknowledge my debt to these publishers, as also to *The Furrow* (Maynooth, Ireland), which has published preliminary and subsequent explorations of some of the themes brought together in this book.

Part I
The Visionary Worlds of St Teresa of Avila

THE WOMAN AND THE ANGEL

i. *A Cartesian Prologue*
Teresa de Cepeda y Ahumada, known in her religious
persona as Mother Teresa of Jesus, and in her historical
persona as St Teresa of Avila, was born in 1515, the year that
Martin Luther, in another part of the Holy Roman Empire,
had his liberating Tower experience; and died in 1582, the
same year in which Protestantism fully defined and
consolidated itself.

It is with Teresa that these meditations are concerned, but
it is well to bear in mind the larger historical stage against
which her life was set, and to remember how much she was
in fact affected, especially in her darker moments, by the
Lutheran upheaval. She seems to have been much less affected
by that other great event which spanned her life, the discovery
of the Americas, even though her family was fairly deeply
involved in its dark and dubious consequences. Basically,
she saw both events as a challenge to that Light of Christ
which Spain represented, the Spain of a true reformation of
religious and Christian life. Not so much Spain as we know
it, rather a Spain centred in and almost identified with
Castile. She was a woman deeply rooted in her own place
and time. She was also a woman who received illumination
from that spirit-world that reaches upwards to the Divine
source of life and love. An understanding of her visions must
take account of both sets of co-ordinates.

Perhaps the word 'co-ordinate' may strike the right note to introduce briefly a very great man, in his way a good and godly man, who was born fourteen years after the death of Teresa, a certain Monsieur du Perron, better known as René Descartes. It was he who invented the geometry of co-ordinates in order to plot and plan, and reduce to order the seemingly disordered manifold of the universe. Thus he would bring the whole world within the human mind, the lonely mind of man that at the beginning of Descartes' famous meditations seemed shut into itself. For Descartes was the first great Western thinker to step out of the Divine radiance into the world of the human subject as the only real ground of certainty. This ancient radiance, in which both Augustine and Aquinas stood, was full of light, of regions and hierarchies open to the visionary, open to a Catherine of Siena, a Francis of Assisi, a Julian of Norwich, as it had been open to the writers of the Old Testament and the New. Unless we clearly understand that this world was open and available to Teresa of Avila we shall make nothing of her visions.

Descartes stepped out of this radiance, or more correctly he saw that this radiance had faded from the minds of his contemporaries, and with it the sense of concepts as luminaries to guide us rather than bricks to build with. He had to find the light within his mind, and from there, from this one point of light, open up to a fully transcendent light which could stand as the vital source of all knowledge. It is this quest which gives its immense intellectual tension to his *Discourses* and *Meditations*. It was all very much in the head, very much in the crystalline world of intelligence, which thus stood over against the material world as totally other. So it came about that nowadays we can think of only two regions of reality: matter and spirit, or body and soul, and are quite unable to grasp the ontology of an author like

St Teresa who is quite innocent of that assumption, for whom there are many regions of reality between physical matter and the region of pure spirit.

It is against this background that we must read the texts with which these meditations are concerned. Those who have either a monistic view of the world as matter merely or spirit merely, or who work with a dualism of spirit and matter, will never understand these texts, nor the meditations based on them. Nor will any criticisms coming from any of these sources have any real validity.

ii. *The Fiery Dart*

We must understand, then, that Teresa was commonly in touch with a special region inhabited by beings called 'angels', a region which was also open to the writers of the New Testament. This region was neither imaginary in the way Tolkien's Middle-Earth is imaginary or Ursula Le Guin's Earthsea is imaginary. Neither is it a world of physical perception, as for example, the world of UFO sightings. Even if an UFO phenomenon disappears abruptly and mysteriously, nevertheless it is seen as a physical object in the physical world. Teresa's angel-world is neither imaginary nor physically real. Yet it is seen as real, and as having a real effect on people's lives, especially on Teresa's own life. Sometimes this reality has definite shape, form and colour; in this case it is called, rather confusingly, an *imaginary* vision: a better term would be an image-vision. Sometimes it is merely felt or experienced in a general way; even more confusingly, this is called an *intellectual* vision. For Teresa both types of experience are an encounter with a real world.

Usually angels were present to Teresa as presences in an intellectual vision. We are not directly concerned here with this kind of contact with the angels, but with a very vivid, dramatic and celebrated image-vision, that of the angel with the golden arrow or dart. This vision has been made the subject of a famous picture by Bernini, and the picture in turn called forth Richard Crashaw's celebrated poem, 'The Flaming Heart'. All this is based on a single paragraph at the end of Chapter 29 of Teresa's autobiography, or *Life* as it is called, which runs as follows:

> Sometimes I would see an angel near me, at my left side, in bodily shape . . . not great but quite small, and very beautiful, with such a glowing countenance that it seemed to be one of those very exalted angels that are all on fire . . . In his hands he held a great golden dart, and the tip of the metal seemed to be aflame. He penetrated my heart several times with this dart, and it seemed to search out my inmost depths. Indeed as he withdrew the dart it seemed as if my very entrails followed it, and I remained totally on fire with a great love of God. So great was the pain that I cried out several times, and so much greater was the sweetness which was the result of this pain that one could not take it away no matter how one tried; nor is one satisfied with aught less than God Himself. This is not a physical pain but a spiritual one; yet the body does share it, and sometimes very strongly.[1]

The first thing to notice about this vision is that it was not a unique experience. The text of the *Life* says it happened *algunos veces* 'several times' or 'sometimes'. We know from another Carmelite source that the experience occurred not only around the period described in the *Life* but also much later, about ten years before Teresa's death. It seems then to be a kind of signature of the mystical experience or mystical *persona* of Teresa. It is not strange, therefore, that the experience has been favoured by the institution of a special feast in her Church, like Paul's

[1] *Vida* Ch. 29. Here as in other passages quoted from St Teresa's writings I have made my own translation, using the Aguilar (Silverio) edition, (Madrid, 1957).

experience on the road to Damascus and Francis's experience of the wounds of Christ.

The next thing to notice is that the experience was at once spiritual and physical. Yet it is primarily spiritual, and only physical or corporeal by participation. The fiery dart is not the kind that could cause a physical wound; in its essential nature it is of spirit-stuff or soul-stuff, and its essential purpose is to wound Teresa interiorly. Yet this wound is not merely a mental event, and so we are forced to look carefully at the conception of a spiritual body which is at once both spiritual and corporeal.

The third observation is a very obvious one, and has been noted frequently, especially by those who wish to reduce the experience to terms of hysteria and self-delusion. This is the fact that the whole experience is strongly erotic in its imagery, in what is said to happen and in the whole atmosphere of the passage. It was surely one of the passages singled out for special splutterings by those honest fellows who wanted all Teresa's works consigned to the flames after her death.

In what follows we shall look at these three points in turn, beginning with the second, going on to the third, and finishing with a few words about the first.

iii. *The Heart in its own Place*

Teresa's vision as she describes it makes no kind of sense unless we assume the real existence of what I have termed 'the spiritual body'. The term is, of course, taken from St Paul (1 Corinthians 15), for whom the spiritual body is the resurrection body that is related to the visible physical body as the seed is to the plant that grows from it. Here we are not concerned with the resurrection body but with a reality that is present here and now, a reality that may well survive death or else is transformed at death, a reality that is at once invisible and yet full of life and feeling. It is in the world of this reality that the heart of Mary was pierced, according to Simeon's prophecy. It was in the world of this reality that the blood and water flowed from the pierced side of Jesus on the Cross. It is in the world of this reality that Paul is able to say that he lives now not in his own life but in the life of Christ. This last statement cannot be understood in physical visible terms, but neither is it a mere metaphor: it tells of a real life and a real flowing, as real as the piercing of the heart of St Teresa.

It is of course possible that the phenomena of this intermediate region may have repercussions at the visible physical level. This is clearly stated by Teresa herself. And of course her heirs and successors in the Carmelite Order took the phenomenon of the Transverberation so physically that they claim that a rent or split was apparent in her physical heart after death; in fact this rent is said to be still visible in her heart preserved in a casket in Avila. But at best the rent in the physical heart could be seen only as a repercussion from the real wound, which was dealt and received at another level.[2]

It must be remembered that ancient and medieval philosophy distinguished three levels in man, the vegetative, sensitive and intellective. These were called *animae*, which is normally translated 'soul', but might be more accurately rendered as 'levels of life', since the *anima* was not a spiritual entity in our post-cartesian sense but rather a principle of life: thus every plant has its own *anima*.

So there is nothing new or particularly esoteric in talking of an inner or intermediate or 'spiritual' body in which

[2] It is conceivable that the 'spiritual' body may have so affected the corruptible visible body that this latter does not go its own way at death, so that we have the well-attested phenomenon of incorruptibility attributed for instance to the remains of St Bernadette of Lourdes. This phenomenon was also attributed to St Teresa's remains.

organs such as the heart, and elements such as blood, can be distinguished. What is to be stressed is that these organs and elements are not metaphorical but real, so that when Teresa speaks of her heart and entrails being pierced and transformed into fire she is using words carefully and literally in the context of this inner level of life.

Now the pierced heart of the woman is what may be called a Christian archetype. Such archetypes are realities beyond or above time which are in varying circumstances and degrees verified or incarnated in human history. The most central Christian archetype is that of the suffering servant of God, and this is also found reflected more or less brokenly outside Christianity, in Plato's presentation of Socrates, for example, or in the Yoruba history or legend of Ayelala, the King's daughter who dies for her people. There is a whole cluster of archetypes here, changing one into the other, and indeed Ayelala crying out as her heart breaks brings us to Mary and Simeon's prophecy fulfilled in the woman standing beside the Cross, fulfilled again and again in Christian history. We shall return to this theme shortly, after considering what is called the erotic quality of Teresa's vision.

iv. *The Holy Force*
When writers like Professor Leuba[3] say that the passage we are examining is erotic rather than mystical, our answer is neither to deny that it is erotic nor even that it is both erotic and nevertheless mystical, but rather to say that it is

[3] J. H. Leuba, *The Psychology of Religious Mysticism* (Routledge and Kegan Paul, London, 1925 (reprinted 1972)) pp. 144ff. Professor Leuba, William James and Fr Ronald Knox have between them had immense influence in imposing a negative, and ultimately puritanical, image on the affective and bridal mystical experience of Christian men, and especially Christian women mystics. They are worth reading as countering the exaggerations of some of the less prudent mystics. For a more positive and balanced approach one should go to writers like Henri Brémond, Von Hügel and Louis Cognet.

erotic precisely because it is mystical. However, one must hasten to add that the *eros* in question here is not a self-indulgent or possessive *eros*, not *eros* off on its own destructive course, Plato's sensual *eros* unaccompanied by intellectual *eros*. It is rather a question of that basic and all-pervasive vital force in man and woman which is the energy of creation, whose truth is always creativity, whose joy is true to itself only when it is creative. This holy force is at the root of all reverence and all true religion.

This holy force has indeed been misused, misunderstood, vulgarised, trivialised, and distorted into montrous perversions of its true eternal beauty by fallen man. Indeed there is truth in the ancient tradition that man fell through the misuse of this sacred power. And those who maintain, with Luther, Kierkegaard and Barth, that human nature was totally defaced and depraved by the fall will regard all human *eros* as we know it and feel it as the place of evil. From the point of view of this theology all humankind can do is be invaded by the heavenly *agapé* which placed all expression of the natural man under the sign of condemnation. From this point of view a passage such as that we are concerned with here is an abomination. It is no wonder then that this form of theology repudiates all mysticism. This is the negative side of Luther's 'tower experience' of justification by faith alone.

Make no mistake about it, we are here at a parting of the ways. It is by no means the same as the parting of the ways between Protestantism and Catholicism, for on the one hand Protestant thinkers like Schleiermacher and Bonhoeffer are in the last analysis open to mysticism, and on the other many Catholic theologians and Biblical exegetes belong to that anti-mystical spectrum that lies in our day between Barth and Bultmann. No, the line of division has to do with the question of the nature of man, of what man's heart says and feels and the ultimate validity of what man's (and woman's) heart thinks and feels. There is, more especially, the question of the human heart of Christ representing tenderness, longing, loneliness, tears, joy, and exultation.

It is here that Teresa's strong and deep feminine *eros* confronts us, and asks to be fully accepted. The sweep of this feminine *eros* might seem to draw us backward towards sentimentality and self-indulgence. But in truth it sweeps us onwards towards the fulness of self-giving, towards the sacrificial love of Calvary in all its pathos, poignancy and creative power.

Nor must we overlook the radical asceticism of Teresa's life, which served both to sharpen her perception of immaterial reality and to purify and enlarge her sensibility. So, to borrow a phrase from Walter Pater, the whole personality 'burns with a hard gem-like flame'. This is a world, in the words of a more poetic writer 'cold and passionate as the dawn'. Indeed this and not any negative or life-denying animus is the true meaning of Christian asceticism. The Carmelite or other religious who is not a passionate man or woman, should try to summon up enough energy to jump over the wall, and become a civil servant or politician. There is no place for such a one in the vital and colourful world of Teresa.

v. *A Marian Archetype*
Finally, we return to our first observation, that the experience of the angel with the fiery dart was recurrent in Teresa's life and so quite central to the life and work of this woman Doctor of the universal Church. The institution of a feast of the Transverberation is a further indication that the event is seen by the Church to be of permanent significance for Christians.

This significance has to be linked closely to the prophecy of Simeon in St Luke[4] and with the figure of the woman in the Johanine writings; at Cana, at Calvary and in the great vision of the woman clothed with the sun of Revelation 12. This is the archetypal feminine, joyful, sorrowful, and glorious, in the mysteries of bringing forth the new man, the archetypal Adam, and the new world free of darkness and death. This archetype seems to be coming forward insistently in modern times, at Fatima and Beauraing, and above all in the vision of Catherine Labouré in 1830, (which has been presented so powerfully in recent years by that great Marian scholar, René Laurentin) in which the pierced heart of the woman responds to the Christ-heart surrounded by thorns, and the cross is supported by the M that stands for the mystery of the woman.

It is as we relate the transverberation of the heart of Teresa to the prophecy of Simeon that we realise its salvific and cosmic significance. The heart of Teresa becomes a point of contact between man's need for new life and God's fulness of that same life, and from this point of breakthrough that same life streams forth through the time and space of that inner world of the body spiritual. Teresa relives and renews the mystery of virgin motherhood in its angel-piercing and its Christ-fruitfulness. The life that streams forth from her heart reaches us across the centuries as we allow her words to have space within us. She calls us too, gently but strongly, to be ready for our own angel-visitations. She calls us all, men and women, to that bridal receptivity by which, according to our experience and temperament, we open to the Divine Fire and its trans-forming potency. This way is full of joy and peace, but it is not an easy way. It is not the way of bleak and joyless asceticism nor of tight and tense orthodoxy, but it is a way

[4] Teresa herself makes this connection in *Relation* XV.

of total renunciation. Moreover it can mean an encounter with the most terrifying darkness and anguish, as we shall see in the next chapter.

3

A DESCENT INTO HELL

i. *The Dark Fire*

St Teresa gives her account of what came to be called the Transverberation in Chapter 29 of the *Life*, and it is generally dated 1559 when Teresa was forty-five years of age, though, as we have noted, the experience happened to her several times. Over against this celestial experience stands the Saint's experience of her descent into hell, which is described in Chapter 32 of the *Life* and generally dated in the same year.

This is also an experience of Fire. But whereas the fire of Transverberation was, so to speak, the servant or ground of love, life and creative joy, the fire of the descent was the servant of hatred, cruelty and annihilation.

> I felt a fire in the soul, quite impossible to describe. My bodily sufferings were unendurable, and I saw there would be no let-up and no end to them. Yet all this was nothing, simply nothing in comparison with the agony of the soul, so oppressive, so stifling, and with such utter hopelessness of affliction and despair ... If somebody were thus destroying the life of the soul it would be relatively little, but here it is the soul that is tearing itself apart. There is really no way I can describe that inward fire and that despairing torture and torturing despair.[5]

[5] *Vida* Ch. 32, par. 3 and 4. (Aguilar edition). The original Spanish should be read aloud, if one is strong enough to hear it. The language gives a lively sense of constriction and utter desolation.

The whole passage, with its detailed physical description of the hollow in the wall of a deep dark dungeon, is one of the most powerful and terrifying texts in Christian spiritual writing. The ordinary reader who wishes to preserve balance and cheerfulness will almost inevitably find some way of escaping its force, either by putting it down to Teresa's imagination or to some illness of body or mind.[6]

We are not concerned here with this kind of attitude, nor should we wish to prejudge the validity of any of the usual ways of escaping the force of the traditional Christian doctrine of hell. We should rather look squarely at this text, which is by no means out of character in Teresa's writings, and try to provide a sufficiently large space for understanding it within the horizon of the Christian experience of the God of love and life. We shall do this by seeing it reflected in other texts dealing with the same or similar subject-matter.

ii. *The Absence of God*

The first text, which we will return to in Chapter 7, is the description of the Night of Spirit which is to be found in Book II of the *Dark Night of the Soul* of St John of the Cross. In this state, we are told, the soul finds itself in hell 'in the deepest and lowest lake, in dark places and in the shadow of death' (Chapter 6, par. 1); it feels keenly the shadow and woe of death and the pains of hell, which consist in its feeling itself to be 'without God and chastised and cast out' (*ibid*). For John, too, the ground or substance of this experience is Fire, which seems to attack the very centre of the soul.

---

[6] In the *Introduction* to the Penguin Classics edition of the *Life* (1957) the translator J. M. Cohen writes: 'The *unconscious*, in its narrowest connotation, makes occasional incursions into Teresa's thoughts. There is that vision of hell as a narrow muddy passage leading to a cupboard in a wall, which is pure Kafka.'

So far the descriptions of the two great founders of the Reformed Carmel reflect each other with some special points of emphasis either way. But there is one general difference, at first sight a very profound difference. It is this. For Teresa the descent into hell is a divine mercy which shows her her basic sinfulness. 'I understood,' she says, 'that the Lord wished me to see the place which my sins merited and which the demons had prepared for me' *Life* (Chapter 32, par. 1). For John, on the other hand, the experience is, first and last, a way of purification; the dark fire that seems so destructive is in fact absolutely essential in order to cleanse it from 'the rust of (selfish) affections' (*Dark Night* II:6:5). But John tells us that the soul in this state sees none of this positive side of the experience, and only feels that it is in hell hopelessly and eternally. Teresa seems to be describing from the inside the phenomenon which John is describing from the outside, as something recalled and understood. Teresa is a witness, John is a teacher. What is perhaps most of all significant as regards the interpretation of Teresa's experience is John's contention that this kind of experience is absolutely essential if the soul is to be fully purified and divinised.[7]

---

[7] From another point of view authors of the esoteric tradition speak of 'The Guardian of the Threshold', which is a personification of the terror, loneliness and alienation people feel when they face that self-immolation demanded by the mystical call. 'The spiritual being hidden in man, which is man himself, but which he can as little perceive with ordinary consciousness as the eye can see itself, is the guardian of the threshold of the spiritual world.' Rudolf Steiner, *A Road to Self-knowledge* (The Rudolph Steiner Publishing Company, London, 1918), Ch. 4. It must be noted, however, that while Steiner is concerned primarily with knowledge (not excluding love) John is concerned primarily with love (not excluding knowledge). The difference is more than a difference of emphasis; it is a difference of focus. For the reader, who like Steiner himself, lives by the love-principle, Steiner is a treasure-house of wisdom. For the reader or follower who does not live by the love-principle (who, for instance, puts it in the second place) Steiner's writing can be very dangerous.

The second reflecting mirror to place before Teresa's description of her descent into hell is another that we shall consider later, in Chapter 10. It is that passage in the *Story of A Soul* in which St Thérèse of Lisieux describes her state of soul at the end of her life, a state in which she finds herself imprisoned in 'impenetrable darkness'. All her faith in a life beyond death seems to have disappeared completely, and when she tries to reawaken that faith the very darkness itself seems to borrow from the lost souls who live in it the gift of speech and to say: 'It is all a dream this talk of a heavenly country, and of a God who made it all. All right, go on longing for death. But death will only mean a night darker than ever, the night of nothingness (*la nuit du néant*).'[8] And she goes on to say that this description falls far short of what she experiences, that a full description is impossible 'without running the risk of seeming to blaspheme'.

When we recall that Thérèse really lived what she describes, for the last eighteen months of her life when she was often in the greatest physical agony,[9] we realise that we have here a mirror capable of reflecting everything in St Teresa's description. Moreover, we are clearly in the world of St John's 'Dark Night of Spirit' and all it implies of purification and transformation. We realise too that what in the case of others could be worked out over whole decades, was abbreviated and intensified in the case of this young woman who died at the age of twenty-four.

However, there are two points of difference between Thérèse's experience and that of her great Carmelite predecessors. In the first place, where Teresa and John are being crushed by the weight of an angry God, or the weight of their own guilt that cuts them off from the face of

[8] Ch. 32 of Knox translation.
[9] See Guy Gaucher, *Histoire d'Une Vie* (Les Editions du Cerf, Paris, 1982).

God, Thérèse is in the world of the death of God, or rather the nonentity of God. Where she is, there is no God; nor has there ever been. In other words, her hell is a post-cartesian hell, the hell of a generation which no longer stands in the Divine Presence, and which has to find God from within (as Descartes did, and Kant) or not at all. By the time Thérèse was born in the latter half of the nineteenth century, the scientific and materialistic mind had also lost that flicker of light within, and man lived, as he still lives, in a godless world. In this sense Thérèse's experience of hell is much nearer to us than that of St Teresa.

But, and here we come to the second point of difference, Thérèse not only descended into the hell of the godless, she accepted this descent deliberately, as a vicarious atonement. She has been asked by God to sit with the unbelievers and share their 'starvation diet'. She is sitting at a table that has been defiled, and she wishes to cleanse it by her sacrifice; she is sitting in darkness among the unbelievers, so that they (not she) may catch some ray of the faith hidden within her. Thérèse is here the warrior confronting the dragon of unbelief in its darkest lair. This conception of a conflict with Satan in his various forms is, of course, central to the spirituality of Teresa of Avila, and the text we have been looking at must be seen in this context. Her 'place in hell' is the place where she is in the dragon's power, but it is also the place where with God's grace she fights the power of the dragon. It is as we see Teresa reflected in Thérèse that this horizon reveals itself. Here, again, we see the necessity for the descent, not in terms of personal purification alone but in universal or cosmic terms. Those who miss the cosmic dimension run the risk of misunderstanding quite radically the meaning and power of Carmelite mystical writing and experience.

iii. *The Pain of Annihilation*

The next text to use as a reflection of Teresa's text is from a strange and controversial pair of books by the contemporary Irish writer Brian Cleeve : *The House on the Rock* (1978) and *The Seven Mansions* (1980), which the author claims have both been written under direct divine inspiration, the kind of inspiration which Teresa and John of the Cross called interior locution. John indeed warns us repeatedly of the dangers of illusion and deceit to which this kind of spirituality is exposed, and we must bear this in mind in reading Brian Cleeve's testimony. However, there is much in these books of serious and helpful reflection on Christian experience, and this is particularly true of what the books have to say about the mystery of evil, the presence of Satan, and the nature of hell. Briefly, Brian Cleeve's God is a suffering God who seeks to bring all persons and entities back to a community of love, and this includes Satan and all evildoers. But final failure in this is always a possibility. Here is how it is described:

> If that part of creation that turns to evil persists in rebellion to the end, then its existence as a self must cease. Its substance and nature return to their source, which is God. But their selves, their conscious awareness of existing, that will cease to be. That cessation is what men call being damned. It will last only an instant, but an instant in eternity is eternal. Their consciousness of loss, of ceasing to be, will last for ever. And the pain of that consciousness is beyond man's capacity to understand.[10]

It may seem strange to regard annihilation as so terrifyingly painful, since not a few people seem to welcome it. But what they welcome is sleep or unconsciousness or nirvana, which is almost the opposite of

[10] *The Seven Mansions* (Watkins, London, 1980) p. 30. So, too, Henrik Ibsen in *Peer Gynt* sees the annihilation of self-awareness as the ultimate fate of the man who fails in life's purpose, and he tends to eternalise the moment in which Peer Gynt faces this annihilation.

annihilation, since it is a kind of freeing of the self from its narrow confines and a merging with infinity. In the annihilation which is in question here the self has closed all its doors, all possible openings towards the source, and affirms itself as absolute and utterly alone. A contemporary philosopher, Emmanuel Levinas, has written a book of which the theme is that 'Being is exteriority'.[11] By being he means human consciousness, and his thesis is that it is only by going out of itself towards others that consciousness exists: to remain within is to cease to exist. Yet consciousness as such, as self-awareness, is not within time but rather creates time by its own functioning. It is true that human consciousness opens out to sleep or nirvana, but this is simply a deepening of awareness as we very well know when we awaken out of a deep sleep. Sleep is always cradled in cosmic awareness.

To face annihilation on the other hand is to come up against a wall that reaches to the sky, to face a desert that has no end, to enter a darkness that has rejected all light. Here there is neither sleep, nor rest, nor hope, nor love. From this point of view to be taken into hell is to be given some share in this intolerable ever-wakeful despair. Perhaps it has happened and can happen that some strong souls are brought into this place precisely in order that some light may shine in this total darkness, and that those trapped within it may find the beginnings of a way out; a spark of humble love falls on them to save them, if only they receive it. This is the truth and power of the descent of Christ into hell, something, like everything he does, shared in some measure by those who truly follow him. In a sense the greatest Christian mystery is the harrowing of hell, as the great Christian sign is the sign of Jonah. This was and is the

---

[11] *Totalité et Infini* (Martinus Nijhoff, La Haye, 1971).

mystery of the first Christian Sabbath, the mystery of Holy Saturday.

No less terrible than annihilation is absolute loneliness. It is this prospect of final loneliness that makes some old people terrified of hospital, and that is the main ingredient of certain tortures where the victim is alone with his pain and forsaken by God and man precisely because there is no one there to answer his cry for help. Indeed a contemporary theologian, Hans Urs von Balthasar, describes hell as the complete loneliness of being-only-for-oneself. And he goes on to say that 'God himself enters this loneliness as one who is even more lonely, so that what we call hell, although a place of desolation is still a Christological place'.[12]

We are here at the heart of the mystic's descent into hell, and at the heart of the experience described so vividly by St Teresa. The mystic follows Christ the whole way, and in doing so pushes the mystery of redemptive love to its limits. When he is within this place, the mystic does not at all realise that it is a Christological place. It is only from the outside that he and we realise this. The mystic rests in the hollow of the Father's hand. But so does the spirit that has totally excluded God. Because hope and faith and love lie dormant but really present within the mystic, there is, to our human vision, the possibility of a mighty work of final reconciliation, that 'Great Deed' of which Blessed Julian speaks, the final triumphant harrowing of hell.[13]

[12] Curiously, von Balthasar's writing on hell is based on the experienced 'descent into hell' of the twentieth-century mystic, Adrienne von Speyr (1902–67), whose visionary world is the context of all von Balthasar's theology. This is the first time in the history of theology that a major theologian has based his system on private revelation. It is a powerful system based, however, on a dangerous precedent; for easy or cheap knowledge is harmful to men and women.

[13] *Revelations of Divine Love*. It must be remembered that for Mother Julian there is in every human being 'a godly will that never assented to sin' (Ch. 37).

4

'THE HUMAN FORM DIVINE'

i. *'A Perilous Road'*

Perhaps the most important moment of decision in the spiritual journey of Teresa of Avila was that described as follows in Chapter 22 of the *Life*, her first and most complete account of the stages of that journey.

> When I began to gain some experience of mystical prayer, that is to say at the level of a quiet resting with God, I used to manage to put aside all bodily images, even though I did not dare to look upward to the Divinity. I was so constantly conscious of my wickedness that to look upwards seemed the height of presumption. All the same, I seemed to be experiencing the presence of God, and in fact I was; and I was able to remain with Him in a state of recollection. This is indeed a joyful way of prayer, as long as God is in it; and it brings great delight. And because of this spiritual gain and pleasure, there was no way I would turn to the Humanity of Christ, for truly it seemed to me to be an impediment.[14]

Her recollection of her attitude during this period changed somewhat by the time she came to write the *Interior Castle* twelve years later. It was not so much that she had turned away from the Humanity of Christ as that she took less joy (*gusta*) in thinking of him, and went about in a kind of absorption, guarding an inner glow (*regalo*), the 'delight' she speaks of in the passage from the *Life*. It is noticeable that she speaks in quite a different tone of the

[14] Ch. 22, par. 3 (Aguilar edition).

26

positive content of this state of prayer in her later description. The impression left by the description in the *Life* is that this imageless state brought her both joy and gain, and that God was in it; the description of it in the later work is dismissive and almost sarcastic.

What she is quite clear about in both texts is that the negative aspect of this state was quite wrong and even dangerous. It was a kind of betrayal – 'high treason' (*gran traición*) in fact – though done in ignorance. It was, she tells us in the *Interior Castle* 'a perilous road', and it could lead to 'a loss of devotion to the Most Blessed Sacrament', not so much directly as through the intervention of Satan. This, indeed, is one of those passages where a shadow falls across the page, the shadow at once of Satan and of the Inquisition. Indeed some of the darkness flows into Teresa's own writing, and the whole passage (in the *Interior Castle*) is minatory and irascible. This shadow is absent from the longer discussion in the *Life*. It is with this discussion we shall be mainly concerned in what follows, treating first of the contemplative aspect of the Saint's affirmation of the Humanity of Christ, its precise import for the activity of contemplative prayer, and in the second place looking at its visionary aspect; for the doctrine is closely bound up with the fact that she had numerous and deep visionary experiences of the Humanity of Christ.

ii. *The Humanity of Jesus Christ*

St Teresa gives two reasons why contemplatives (i.e. Christian contemplatives) should not relinquish the Humanity of Christ. The first is 'a small fault in the matter of humility' (*un poco de falta de humildad*) which causes the soul to raise itself before the Lord raises it, and to leave behind something so precious as the Humanity of Christ. This, Teresa adds, is trying to be Mary before one has laboured with Martha.[15] She does not press this point, and is content with calling it a kind of mote in the eye, here as elsewhere adapting a scriptural image to her own purposes.

Obviously the point is valid only if it is assumed that the contemplation of the Humanity of Christ belongs to the level of discursive meditation (the Martha level), an assumption made by her opponents but not accepted by Teresa. So it is that she can say a few pages on that the contemplation of the Humanity of Christ belong to the Mary level, which is that of infused or (as Teresa calls it) 'supernatural' contemplation. It must be remembered that the distinction between meditation or active contemplation, on the one hand, and infused or supernatural or mystical contemplation, on the other, is the hinge on which everything turns in our author's spiritual doctrine. It is only in the latter type of contemplation that God takes over, and the rain begins to fall abundantly on the soul. For Teresa, the contemplation of Christ's Humanity belongs *also* and fully at this higher stage, though here she is admitting 'for the sake of argument' her opponents' principle that meditation is left behind at the doorway into higher or infused contemplation. However, this raises the whole question of what Teresa means by meditation, and we shall look at this presently.

This then is the first difficulty (*inconveniente*) in the position that Teresa is attacking, the position of those who would speedily leave behind all corporeal images including that of the Humanity of Christ. The second is more serious, and Teresa puts it sharply and clearly. 'We are not angels and we have bodies. It is quite ridiculous (*desatino*) to play the angel while we are on the earth, especially as earth-bound as I was' (i.e. at the time she took this false

[15] *Life* Ch. 22, par. 9 (Peers edition p. 140). All quotations in this section are from Ch. 22 of the *Life* unless otherwise indicated.

path). Since we are on the earth we need an *arrimo*, something to lean on, especially in times of stress or aridity. At such times Christ is a very good friend and companion. Our author admits however, here as elsewhere, that there may be times when the soul is indeed taken beyond all corporeal images and when Christ withdraws himself. This he does, she adds, in order 'to draw the soul out of itself' (*sacar el alma de si*) so that it is 'full of God' (*plena de Dios*).

We have to be careful here. At first sight it looks as if we are being told that this state is a passing one, and also that it is a higher one, higher that is than that in which the Humanity of Christ is present. If Teresa were to concede that it is a higher state (as seems indicated by the phrase 'full of God') she would in fact be conceding the entire case to her opponents, for they were simply asserting that souls who are advancing should not be kept back to the level of corporeal images, but should indeed go out of themselves to God and be filled with God. We know that John of the Cross expended many pages of invective in his *Living Flame of Love* on directors who would hold back at the level of discursive meditation those who were being called onwards to a higher way of prayer.[16] Is Teresa, after all, opting for a kind of debilitating prudence in the name of humility and a facile realism, the kind of realism of the down-to-earth person which Aristotle rejected long ago when, in that marvellous passage at the end of the *Nicomachean Ethics*, he holds that a man should follow 'the divine something' that raises him up to contemplation?

[16] Stanza 3. This is not the place to tackle the problem, much explored by writers such as Baruzi and Truman Dicken, as to whether there is a basic difference in this matter between Teresa and John. Certainly there is a difference of emphasis and highlight; perhaps the present book may help to throw some light on the question as to whether there is a deep rift of principle between the two great Carmelite writers.

We shall return to this question in a moment. For the present it will suffice to note that our author is affirming the way of the Humanity of Christ as the staple of contemplative prayer, while allowing a secondary place to another state in which, for a short period, the Humanity of Christ is transcended.

The question that must be faced at this point, and which has been with us all along, is that of the precise meaning of the presence of Christ's Humanity in prayer, the meaning it has, that is to say, for St Teresa.

A close reading of the text – the main passage in the *Life* and the shorter account in the *Interior Castle* – reveals three quite distinguishable and indeed distinct strands in Teresa's understanding of the Divine Humanity, the 'human form divine' of the Son of Man. (The phrase is from Blake, for whom every human body is 'divine', but obviously it can be applied with special force in the case of the human presence of the Word made flesh.)

The three strands may be named in terms of presence as: 'presence-before', 'presence-beside' and 'presence-below', or Christ as object of contemplation, Christ as friend and companion, and Christ as support. Reading the text carefully we see now one strand, now another coming to the fore and giving way to the others like an unwinding rope. So, for instance in the paragraph with which we have been just now concerned, that in which Teresa gives her second argument against her opponents, we see the different strands come and go as we read on (Peers, pp. 140, 141). The Divine Humanity is first an object for our thoughts: 'presence-before', then a friend (*amigo*) and companion (*compania*) who is at our side: 'presence-beside', then a supporting hand that helps us to rise when we fall: 'presence-below'. The same pattern shows itself throughout: Christ present as object of meditation, Christ present as companion-friend, Christ present as final and utterly trustworthy support and enablement (*arrimo*).

Now Teresa's opponents would fully accept the second and third strands of her affirmations. As Christian contemplatives they would not only accept but quite categorically affirm the absolute necessity of the presence of the total Christ, man and God, as companion and support. Teresa is here pushing an open door, yet it is here that she in fact pushes her arguments most strongly.

The matter is different when we look closely at the first strand in our author's affirmation: the presence of the Divine Humanity as the object of contemplation. The whole Dionysian tradition of the Divine darkness, most powerfully expressed in the English fifteenth-century text the *Cloud of Unknowing*, would lead the contemplative at a certain stage – which in fact the author of the *Cloud* is careful to identify – beyond all images and symbols into a world of complete darkness which can only be pierced by 'a naked intent' of total love of God. Much in St John of the Cross goes in the same direction, and clearly this kind of approach was quite common in St Teresa's time. Indeed it is clear from the *Interior Castle* that what she had written in the *Life* had been strongly challenged.[17]

However, we must be very careful to try to define what exactly St Teresa is saying. She is *not* saying that the imagined lineaments of Jesus of Nazareth must be always before the inner eye of the mind: none of her language is quite physical in this sense. All the examples she gives have to do with events in the life of Jesus which show us the divine *mysteries* being worked out in pictorial terms: a man sitting by a well, a man being stripped of his garments and scourged, above all a man rising in splendour from the tomb. (Let it be noted that we are here trying to isolate that

[17] *Interior Castle* VI.7 (Peers p. 324).

first strand in our author's affirmation, since frequently
even when she is speaking of the events of Christ's life she
is also seeing him as companion or support.) In these cases
the pictured image is no more than a bridge or a reminder
of the general presence of Christ in Christian contemplation.

Let us look more closely at these images of events which
bring Christ before the inner eye as the object of
contemplation. We have said that event and image must be
seen in the context of the divine mysteries, in the general
context of the mystery of the Incarnation. And it is in this
context that we must take up the question of meditation,
and why it is that Teresa seems both to agree with John of
the Cross that it must be left firmly behind as the soul
advances, and yet seems to reject any complete disengage-
ment of the mind from the world of corporeal images, at
least as represented by the Humanity of Christ.

The key text here is to be found in the same chapter of
the *Interior Castle* with which we have been concerned,
Chapter 7 of Book VI. It comes up in fact by way of an
elucidation of what is meant by meditating on the
Humanity of Christ; and it centres on a distinction which
is itself not very clear at first reading. Peers translates the
key sentence as follows (p. 306): 'You know, of course,
that it is one thing to reason with the understanding
(*discurrir con el entendimiento*) and quite another for the
memory to represent truths to the understanding (*repre-
sentar la memoria al enterdimiento vendaderas*)'. What is
not quite clear in Peers' translation is that the key word is
discurrir, which involves a step by step activity; this is clear
from the three examples which follow: the first is an
intellectual process of reflexion on the Incarnation, the
second an imaginative reconstruction of the events of the
Passion, the third a focussing on the details of one incident
of the Passion, again by way of imagination. All this is

fairly clear in itself, but it may not be so clear how we can go beyond this kind of meditation, and yet stay with the Humanity of Christ as the primary object of contemplation. In fact the paragraph in which she explains the other side of her distinction demands very careful reading, for here too we are asked to look pictorially or imaginatively at Christ, in this case Christ on his knees in the Garden; and we have to ask how this differs from discursive meditation as represented by the third example already given, that of taking one episode of the Passion and meditating on it in detail.

Are we not in the second case meditating in detail on the episode of the Agony in the Garden? Not so. Here there is question of an interior glance, a kind of intuition, a mere look (*de solo ver*), a simple vision (*una sencilla vista*). This mere look is, if one may use the image, the launching pad of the mind's journey into the world of Divine mystery, a world in which the mind is at this stage entirely at home. What has happened is that the memory has brought an image before the understanding which launches the understanding into the heavens of contemplation, a world which may be full of light or in deepest darkness. Indeed (though our author does not make this point) here the mystical darkness that covered the soul of Christ in Gethsemane may in some measure surround us as we open out to the Divine mystery. What Teresa is most concerned with affirming is that the whole prayer-experience, already fed by the mystical flowing from on high, should be grounded in the Incarnation, should be itself deeply incarnate. Once this anchoring in the Word made flesh is affirmed fully and concretely, there is no limit to the horizons of contemplative vision.

It is worth noting that for Teresa the Liturgy has a vital presence in this process: the seasons and festivals of the

Christian year become full of light and significance. Indeed all the music and pageantry of the Liturgy are in no way distractions from the contemplative experience, but rather serve to articulate it and reflect it. So it can happen that a scriptural or traditional phrase may echo within the mind for days, and serve as a kind of vantage-point from which immense vistas open out. At the level of discursive meditation the Liturgy is precious and valid, and can arouse delight and fervour as well as tears and a deep communion with the sorrowful mysteries. But that inner world of deep substantial peace and joy in the midst of, sometimes, utter darkness, in the midst of, sometimes, contention with the powers of darkness: this tremendous world of what Teresa calls 'supernatural' prayer is still waiting to reveal itself. When it begins to reveal itself any holding back at the pedestrian step by step level becomes a heavy debilitating burden. The soul wants to fly upwards and leave the earth and all its sheer plod behind, going into a wide serene beyond all earthly images. Even when this sheer plod involves the events in the life of Christ and uses the imagery of 'Christ's human form divine', it can hold back and hold down the soul. It is an easy step from this to saying that at a certain level of prayer there is no need any more for recourse to the Divine Humanity of Christ. This step Teresa refuses to take. But the last thing she would want is that people should be forced back to pedestrian ways of prayer. Unfortunately her words have sometimes been taken in this sense by superiors and spiritual directors, who neither distinguish the various strands in her teaching on this matter, nor understand that she is speaking as a mystic and for those who have crossed the frontier of infused contemplation.

iii. *The Visionary Aspect*

It is impossible to separate St Teresa's doctrine on the presence of Christ's Humanity in contemplative prayer from her visionary experiences of the same Divine Humanity. These were frequent and various, consoling and disconcerting, intimately personal and yet as an essential part of that shared spiritual experience which is the burden of her writings. For some readers they are the clearest indication of the value and validity of her life and teachings; for others they are the expression of deep unconscious drives and tensions, and indicate a pathological condition which puts her whole witness in question; for others still – and this is probably the average reaction – they are a kind of personal and cultural extra which has little or nothing to do with the saint's doctrines or achievements, and which are best ignored or passed over lightly in presentations of her teaching. In the few pages that follow we shall not try to deal directly with this general problem, nor start with assuming any of these positions, but rather try to understand what part this visionary presence of Christ played in her attitude to the question of the presence of the Divine Humanity in contemplative prayer.

The main 'visions' text follows on from the discussion of the Divine Humanity in Chapter 22 of the *Life*, and these experiences may be said to be the main theme of the succeeding ten chapters, not least because her visionary experiences become the occasion of discussion and disagreement between Teresa and her spiritual guides. It is quite clear from this narrative that she did her very best to find 'another and more secure path',[18] and that in spite of all her efforts her visionary experiences persisted.

[18] Ch. 27, par. 1. *por otro camino que puesse mas saguro*. We must remember that this was the time of the Inquisition and that many visionaries came under its

The visions were mainly of Christ, and these are set down especially in Chapters 27, 28 and 29. They are, as has been said, frequent and various, but one thing is common to all of them: they are not seen with bodily eyes; they are not in the everyday sense corporeal. 'Neither this nor any other vision did I see with corporeal eyes, but rather with the eyes of the soul (*los ojos del alma*).'[19] It is clear that Teresa makes a sharp distinction between the everyday world and the world of her visions; she does not mix the two, and this gives balance and sanity to her whole character. (It is precisely such a confusion that makes the visions of neurotics so distressing and at times so destructive.)

There is a further distinction which is equally important: that between the world of imagination or fantasy and the world of vision. St Teresa is quite clear and categorical about this: what she sees in her visions is quite distinct from the kind of thing that can be imagined. As we have seen she is quite willing to use the imagination in both discursive and mystical meditation, and we have to be careful in the latter case especially to distinguish what is seen 'in the mind's eye' from what is seen 'by the eyes of the soul'. In the former case the image is called up, kept under the control of the mind, and so can be dismissed at will. In the latter case the image is given and remains for a

Continued from page 35.

hammer and were destroyed. There is a kind of massive assumption both in St Teresa's writings and in the writings of Catholic historians and commentators that these other visionaries who were condemned and destroyed were deluded or depraved. But this assumption is wide open to challenge. Indeed it could be argued that Teresa's emergence as a light to future generations may well be bound up with the blood and tears of her fellow-visionaries who were imprisoned and sometimes tortured and murdered in the name of orthodoxy. It may be well to add that the assumption of some non-Catholic authors that *all* these visionaries were neurotic is equally obtuse.

[19] Ch. 27, par. 4.

certain time; it cannot be dismissed, nor can it be recalled at will once it has gone. One can of course recall it as an imagined image in speaking about it or writing about it, but this brings us back to our former case.

What can cause confusion is that our author calls some of her visions 'imaginary' inasmuch as they come before the mind in clear images. Let us look at a description of this experience of an imaginary vision of the Humanity of Christ. It will be found towards the beginning of Chapter 28 of the *Life*.

> One day when I was at prayer the Lord was pleased to show me his hands, hands of most marvellous beauty . . . A few days later I saw the divine countenance as well, and the whole experience left me completely absorbed . . . You might think that it took no great force to see hands and countenance of such beauty. But glorified bodies are of such a nature that their beauty, when we see it mystically, quite overcomes us . . . When I was at Mass on the feast of St Paul I saw the whole of that most sacred Humanity as it is represented in paintings of the Resurrection full of beauty and majesty.

It is difficult to escape the impression that this vision of the Humanity of Christ breaks through the normal conventions and is an apotheosis of the human form divine in its masculine mode. The whole atmosphere is one of quite extraordinary reverence. Reversing Wordsworth's image in his sonnet 'On Calais Beach' we can say that this woman 'breathless with adoration' is a great world of earth and sea and sky, the perfect setting and receptacle for the Perfect Man as He walks in total presence, power and beauty: the feminine seeing is as real as the masculine seen, and the one cannot be separated from the other. In other words, we cannot ask what is *there* objectively, nor yet can we call the experience subjective, as if it merely proceeded from Teresa's state of heightened awareness. Rather is it an authentic happening within the world of the feminine-mystical in which the vital energies are transformed into seeing and loving, and a new kind of being. We have a parallel in the Marian visions of St Bernard and of some other men mystics. Nevertheless it must be remembered that the true mystic is always androgynous, always both masculine and feminine, and so we can have both types of vision for both men and women, though the basic signature of gender remains. Again, it must be recalled that the imaginary visions are neither corporeal nor the work of imagination: they are seen as *given*, bringing with them great gifts of peace and strength, and a sharper realism in dealing with the everyday world.

These imaginary visions are pictorial, seen in terms of contour and colour: had Teresa been an artist she could no doubt have drawn and painted what she saw. Intellectual visions on the other hand are not pictorial, having neither shape nor colour. Yet these visions are somehow concrete, and are located in time and space. Here is how she describes such a vision of Christ's Humanity in Chapter 27 of the *Life*:

> It was the feast of the glorious St Peter; I saw beside me, or rather sensed (for I saw nothing either with the eyes of the body or the eyes of the soul) that Christ was beside me, quite close to me; and it seemed to me that he was speaking to me . . . I felt that Jesus Christ went along with me at my side, though since it was not an imaginary vision I did not have any picture of him. But he remained all the time at my right side. This I felt very clearly and also that he was a witness to all that I did.

And she goes on to say that this vision was full of light, not physical or visible light (as in the imaginary visions) but rather the light of a knowledge 'brighter than the sun'. Moreover, it must be distinguished from the sense of the presence of God which is commonly present in all mystical prayer.

It is worth recalling here the distinction made earlier between 'presence-before' and 'presence-beside'. In Teresa's imaginary visions the Divine Humanity is a 'presence-before', an object of love and contemplation; in the intellectual visions Christ is a 'presence-beside', a companion who witnesses all she does. The two modes of presence echo quite strongly the normal relationship between man and wife in a happy marriage: the partners love one another and variously mirror and create new life in each other; they also work together in making a home and maintaining it, and, it may be, in bringing up a family. It is no accident that Teresa's awareness of the Heavenly Bridegroom takes these two forms, or that she has to fight for the reality of her awareness against men and demons. Neither is it strange that she has been called hysterical by some commentators, for hysteria arises from the demands of the *hyster* or womb when other demands are denied or misdirected: they are the cry of the woman whose womanhood is in pain. We know from Teresa's auto-biography that what happened within her consciousness deeply and dramatically affected her bodily states, that news, for example, of the possibility of a new foundation quickly cured a state of extreme prostration. In a sense she comes across as the type of the hysterical woman, in whom inner needs and sorrows largely determine her physical state and her ability to cope with life's challenges.

Yet Teresa did cope with life's challenges and did so quite magnificently. This is abundantly clear from her letters. Not only does she cope with situations which would have quite flattened most of us, for instance the direction of a complex system of religious foundations which had her writing letters late at night after an exhausting day, but she did so with marvellous grace and subtlety and a serene lightness of touch. Though she is sometimes severe, sometimes weary, sometimes (it must be said) manipulative, yet she is never heavy. She is first and last the perfect mother, the woman in whom there has been, in agony and ecstasy, in labour and joy, the perfect fulfilment of the womb. Her 'hysteria' is not the cry of a womb unfulfilled but the alleluia of Mary and Elizabeth, the Virgin Daughter of Sion who becomes the mother of a new world.

Teresa's visions are as real as her mystical marriage, and her mystical marriage is as real as its fruitfulness in her life of prayer and in the work of prayer she mothered. And this reality of the Virgin Daughter of Sion who is Mother of Carmel is as real today as it was in the sixteenth century, for it is of a stuff that is timeless and enduring.

iv. *Questions Arising*
At the end of this meditation on St Teresa's experience of the Divine Humanity a whole sheaf of themes for further meditation begins to appear. There is, arising from what we have just observed, the theme of Virgin-Motherhood as the true cosmic motherhood of which ordinary motherhood of one or two, or even ten children is but a faint image: there is the need also to speak out loud and clear in defence of this ancient Christian ideal which a materialistic generation no longer understands. It is not a question of saying that the dedicated virgin is better or holier than the wife and mother, but of saying that the ideal of womanhood totally fulfilled not only has naught to do with barren virginity, but immeasurably transcends human marriage and motherhood, which nevertheless provides its only true type and image.

Another meditation taking a slightly different direction would look at 'manwomanhood' as androgyny, the challenge to every man and woman to develop both the feminine and the masculine. Teresa, for all her vibrant and fruitful femity, was in her own phrase a 'strong man' and only by this discovery of her masculine became the great woman she was and is. Branching out from this one could look at the almost forgotten theme of the man in quest of the Holy Grail, the feminine within himself, the way of the mystical marriage and fruitful receptivity, the fulness of fatherhood of which human fatherhood is but an image. Finally, perhaps much further along the road, there would be a meditation on the relationship of individual men and individual women within the world of total dedication to the Kingdom of God.

We shall return to some of these themes later, in Chapters 11 and 12. Here it is appropriate to remind ourselves of the doctrine of Meister Eckhart that Christ is born in each individual Christian who truly and fully opens to his presence. All Teresa's visions of Christ can be seen as moments in this marvellous mystical birth-giving. Like every mystic she is a mirror reflecting the face of the Father. In the words of Sister Elizabeth of the Trinity, she is another humanity in which the Father renews the mystery of the Incarnation. In her and through her Christ lives again, dies again, goes down to hell again, rises again in glory. Her visions of the Humanity of Jesus Christ are simply the expression or overflow of this deep Christian mystery of the continuous Incarnation of Christ in human history. Where so many Christian mystics go upwards to God, Teresa brings God down to earth. So she will always remain within the problems, anxieties and ambiguities of terrestrial existence, as her letters so clearly show. Those who leave the earth for heavenly mansions while still in the body will at some point part company with Teresa. But if they come down from the mount of Transfiguration, as Christ himself did, they will find in Teresa the best of good companions.

5

A VISION OF THE TRINITY

i. *Ways of Seeing*

Let us begin by recalling St Teresa's threefold division of visions according to the faculty which perceives them: corporeal, imaginary and intellectual. *Corporeal visions* reveal themselves to our bodily eyes. Such were the visions or appearances of Christ after the Resurrection. It is generally assumed that St Paul's Damascus Road vision was of this kind. Accounts of ghostly visitations usually claim that something appeared to the physical eyes of the witness or witnesses. Some spiritual people have claimed visionary experiences of this kind, St Bernadette, for example. Perhaps Martin Luther also. Of this kind is the Fatima vision of the sun, though that does not at all mean that the physical sun actually danced and fell towards the earth: the claim can only be that some inner solar reality broke through. Now it must be said clearly that none of Teresa's visions were of this kind. She never saw any vision, corporeal or incorporeal with her bodily eyes.

Imaginary visions are presented to the imagination or inner eye of the soul. This inner perception is very close to external perception, whose images it is forced to borrow to express what it sees. Thus it comes that this kind of vision is always couched in terms of the ordinary experience, religious symbols, cultural mould, and personal idiom of the seer. So it was that Teresa's imaginary visions of angels and saints and demons, of Mary and Christ, were Catholic, Spanish, medieval, and characteristically Teresian. This is not to deny their reality or importance, or their 'givenness', but rather to try to recognise the quality of freedom which links the mystical with the poetic imagination.[20]

There are, in the third place, what Teresa calls *intellectual visions*, which come before the understanding, which are bathed in a light visible neither to the corporeal eye nor yet to the inner eye of the soul. In ordinary everyday vision the eye and the object seen are bathed in a common light, which serves as the medium or womb of the experience. So too in imaginary visions the inner eye and the object seen are bathed in a common light. In both cases the light provides the ground or atmosphere of the experience. In intellectual visions the light itself is the primary content or object of the experience, and any pictorial element is ancillary. However, this class of vision will always assume some kind of theological identity or personality: Christ in one of his mysteries, the Virgin Mary, or one of the saints or angels. Thus there is a theological interpretation of some quality of the light, and usually some accompanying imagery.[21]

---

[20] 'This interior vision comes in an instant like a flash (*relámpago*), and when one least expects it. It brings many good concepts with it, with a very clear inner light, and it moves the will to good desires. Sometimes the concepts and desires come with the vision; sometimes when the vision has departed the soul considers what is the meaning of what it had seen.' J. Gracian, *Peregrinacion de Anastasio*, dialogo quince (Biblioteca Mistica Carmelitana No. 17, Burgos 1933). Strictly speaking what is real and given is the source-experience from which the images flow freely and creatively. See N. D. O'Donoghue 'Mystical Imagination' in J. P. Mackey (ed.) *Religious Imagination* (Edinburgh University Press, Edinburgh, 1986).

[21] 'In this vision there are no shapes or colours as in imaginary visions, but only doctrine and concepts. These are of two kinds: one in which the understanding understands much, and even though they all come together, yet they are distinct one from the other, so that many books could be written from one vision; the other in which only one concept is present which nevertheless encloses many others.' J. Gracian, *loc. cit.*

It is in her intellectual visions that we encounter what may be called the Platonism of St Teresa, that her inner experience finds its place within one of the main intellectual streams of Western thought. Perhaps the best way to see this is to look carefully at a key passage in St Augustine's *Confessions* in which the author sets forth what is arguably his central intellectual discovery, and the doorway to his final conversion experience. The passage will be found in Book VII, Chapter 10, and it relates the experience that came to him through reading the works of Plotinus. It was an experience of entering within himself 'into the depths of my soul'.

> I entered and with the eye of my soul, I saw the light that never changes casting its rays over the same eye of my soul . . . This light was entirely different from any earthly light. It shone above my mind, but not in the way that oil floats above water, or the sky hangs over the earth . . . All who know the truth know this light, and all who know this light know eternity. It is the light that charity knows.

Later on in the *Confessions*, in Book X, Chapter 27, this light is lauded in that wonderful passage which begins 'Late have I loved thee, beauty so ancient and so young, late have I loved thee'.

Here we have the Platonic vision of the Good as mediated by Plotinus, who calls it the One – we have this vision lighting up the whole landscape of the Old and New Testament. One of the most profound qualities of sacred scripture is its power of reflecting all truth in its depths as a lake in the mountains reflects sky and hill-top, house and tree, animals and men. For, after all, the central vision of Plato is but the expression of the very scope and depth of human intelligence.

So it is that as the Unchanging Light (*Lux Incommutabilis*) broke through into the inner sanctuary of mind and heart in Augustine by way of Plato and Plotinus, so it broke through into the inner sanctuary of Teresa's mind and heart directly through the depth, power and pathos of her life of contemplation. What we must ask ourselves is whether it is the same inner world that opens out in the meditation of Plato, Plotinus, Augustine and Teresa. With this quite exciting question in mind let us look at the key text in the *Interior Castle* where she describes her intellectual vision of the Trinity.

ii. *Vision and Doctrine*
The text reads as follows:

> At this point God in his goodness wills to remove the scales from the eyes of the seeker so that he may see something of the gift he has been receiving, even though this he does in a strange manner. The soul is in fact brought into the Seventh Mansions by this experience, which is an intellectual vision wherein, through a kind of figuring forth of the truth, the most Holy Trinity is shown in all its three Persons. There is first a great fire in the spirit after the manner of a cloud of surpassing brightness. Then the soul is given surpassing certainty that the three Persons are one substance, one power, one wisdom and one only God. Thus it comes about that what we have held by faith now we grasp by vision, tho' it is not vision by the eyes of the body nor of the soul, for it is not an imaginary vision. In this experience there is communication and speech from all three Persons, for the soul understands these words of the Lord: that he and the Father and the Holy Spirit will come and dwell in the soul that keeps his commandments.
> (*Interior Castle*, Book VII, Chapter 1)

There are two annotations to this passage made by Teresa's contemporaries. One is by her great friend Fray Hieronymo Gracian, who changes the word 'soul' to 'imagination', so that the key sentence reads: 'It is not a vision by the eyes of the body nor of the imagination'. This brings Teresa's terminology closer to that of Augustine, for whom the highest inner vision is a vision of the soul in the sense of the highest faculty of the soul. In calling her vision intellectual Teresa is in fact agreeing with this, and so Fray Gracian's emendation is helpful.

In another annotation Fray Luis de León explains that there is no question here of the kind of external vision that was given to Moses and St Paul, 'but rather of an infusion of abundant light, accompanied by certain created images. But since these images are neither corporeal nor such as can be grasped imaginatively, the vision is called intellectual and not imaginary.'[22]

Luis de León does not try to explain how an image can be an image and yet not graspable by imagination. However, the word he uses is *especie*, which is the Latin *species*, a word that covers ideas as well as images. An idea is usually accompanied by images, but in itself it is a point of light or luminosity within a general field of light. We may call it a focal point or centering point. Those existentialists and positivists who speak of the dry abstractions of the ancient philosophy simply have no idea of what an idea is. So too those who say we can no longer speak of 'substance', or 'nature', as in transubstantiation theory or natural law theory, simply miss the point: the idea of 'substance' is not like a slab of concrete but rather like a shaft of light. People in those days stood in the Divine radiance, within which it was easy to think and speak in this way. Already in Teresa's time that radiance was fading away into Nominalism or more properly Conceptualism, in which concepts like justification (Luther) and predestination (Calvin) broke away, as the concept of infallibility was later to break away from the Divine irradiation.[23]

---

[22] Aguilar edition, p. 486 note 1.

[23] This is not to question the doctrine, nor for that matter the Christian doctrine of justification, but rather a conceptualistic way of understanding them.

Now what Teresa had at hand, as Luis de León rightly observes, to focus and articulate her greatest vision of God in the soul, was a set of ideas or concepts elaborated by theology over the centuries; a theology of concepts that were not mere conceptions on which the mind could ride wild, but rather points of illumination within the general light of the Divine presence which was also the presence of the Platonic world of unity, truth, being, goodness and beauty.

It would, therefore, seem legitimate to distinguish two moments or elements in the visionary experience related in our text. On the one hand, there is the cloud of surpassing brightness *'una nube de grandisima claridad'* which is the culmination of all the visionary experiences related in the *Life* and the earlier books of the *Interior Castle* (Book VI especially). This experience has its counterpart at various levels in the experiences of mystics of all religious traditions, and is not without a relationship to the philosophical vision of Plato and those in the Platonic tradition. Augustine's *Lux Incommutabilis*, the Unchanging Light above the mind which fills the whole horizon of the spirit suddenly and powerfully, is essentially one and the same light. (We shall return to the question as to whether Augustine's experience is mystical in Teresa's sense.)

On the other hand Teresa's vision is a vision of the Trinity or Triunity, which is described in terms of the most unimpeachable orthodoxy. 'The Holy Trinity is shown in all its three Persons with surpassing certainty so that the soul realises that these three are one substance, one power, one wisdom and one only God.' Obviously there is some floating or attendant imagery here, but essentially the vision at this level is conceptual. It becomes focused in the theological concepts available to Teresa, and this is not difficult since these concepts are in any case points of luminosity within the general radiance of the Divine presence. It is true that these concepts are mediated by faith, but this is a faith that seeks understanding, not a faith that absorbs and swallows all the light of understanding. These theological concepts are servants of the light not masters of it. Teresa's theology does not absorb her vision but rather expresses it. Yet there is a deep affinity between the vision and the theology. It is Teresa, the woman of faith, the sixteenth-century Spanish Catholic Reformer, who has been accorded the vision.

iii. *Light and Fire*

If we were to stop here we should have missed the quality and atmosphere of Teresa's vision of the Trinity. We would be putting knowledge before love, light before fire. We should be seeing Teresa as a Christian thinker, which indeed she was, rather than a Christian mystic which she primarily was and is. Indeed the two should never be separated, but the more disastrous separation is that which cuts away the mystical, or rather the invocational, of which the mystical is a kind of fulfilment and culmination.

So, then, if we look back to our text we shall see that the cloud of surpassing brightness arises by way of a fire in the spirit, *una inflamación que viene a su espiritu*, and we are reminded of the fiery dart of the Transverberation. We are not in the crystalline world of pure intelligence but in the world of the inner heart, the world of that vitality that animates the body and is the very pulse of the blood, yet has its source deep within, invisible to corporeal eyes, yet deeply felt and sometimes causing repercussions in the visible body. This is the place of pathos and poignancy, the place of tears (those sanctifying tears spoken of by Catherine of Siena) the place where, in the words of St

Paul, the Holy Spirit comes to aid us in our invocations, with what the traditional versions used to term 'unutterable groanings'.[24]

Now it is this region within us – let us call it the heart-region – that is for Teresa the ground of all mystical experience, and the preparation for the mystical is a kind of pedagogy of the heart as it strives towards union with God. The *Interior Castle* traces the steps of this pedagogy, its phases, its pitfalls, its basic principles, its point of crisis when ordinary prayer yields place to mystical or, as Teresa calls it, supernatural prayer. The heart is now a garden on which the rain begins to fall, first in drops, then lightly and steadily, then abundantly. Prior to this experience it was as if the garden had been watered laboriously, first by buckets, then by irrigation. A whole new world opens up as the Holy Spirit flows in and abides in the heart.

It is at the culmination of this process that the vision of the Trinity is given to the soul, and the primary purpose of this vision is to reveal to the soul – that is to say to the human heart and mind that is open to God – what has been happening in it. It is as if a fire were active deep down in the heart-region and now bursts forth in flame and light, having consumed all the heavy moistures and rubble of self-love so that it can release itself fully. The fire is indeed the Holy Spirit (as John of the Cross explains in his *Living Flame*), but it reveals also the fulness of the Divinity, and that marvellous *perichoresis* or dance of the three Persons as they affirm their total unity. And they speak to Teresa in words with which she is familiar, words that tell of the promise of the indwelling of all three Persons in all those who follow Christ fully (John 14:23).

[24] Romans 8:26. The NEB translates: 'through our inarticulate groans the Spirit himself is pleading for us'.

The whole visionary and theological aspect of Teresa's experience is secondary to this experience of fire in the heart. But the vision and the theology is none the less real, none the less illuminating, none the less an authentic expression of Christian Platonism. A whole intelligible world opens up, and Teresa accepts it and accepts its conditions. So it was that she would have nothing to do with the rejection of learning and theology which was a feature of the mysticism of the first half of the sixteenth century in Spain. She chose theologians rather than mystics as her counsellors, though she preferred above all else those in whom both were united, as was pre-eminently the case with John of the Cross and Fray Gracian.

In the case of Augustine we find that his journey is first towards the light (culminating in his vision after reading Plotinus) and then towards the fire. When his mind was already filled with the *Lux Incommutabilis* his heart was weighed down with earthly desires, held captive within an egocentric sexuality. The problem was not to escape from sexuality but from egocentricity. This, as we know, happened with his *tolle lege* experience which released this captive energy. One cannot read his eulogies of the Beloved without realising that this was truly a mystical experience in the Teresian sense, an inundation of the whole field of the heart by the inflowing of the Spirit. It is doubtful however whether Augustine ever achieved that full purity and clarity which is the heart-light of the Seventh Mansions. Another way of putting this is to ask whether he ever came to the full possession of his own feminine. But then Teresa only just managed to let go of Fray Gracian (see Chapter 12), and so open the reaches of the masculine within her to the Lord of life and love.

However she does appear to have achieved a basic freedom of heart and with it that purity of feeling and seeing which makes her for all time a sure guide to follow, even though our own way may be very different from hers. Indeed she would – and did – agree entirely with John of the Cross when he said that attachment to visions and other spiritual goods is just as contrary to true spirituality as attachment to earthly goods. Even the indwelling of the Trinity is not a possession to cherish and hold on to but a free celebration of love and life. Moreover, it is certain that the Trinity will dwell in each of us in a unique and personal way, just as Christ will be born in us in a unique and personal way, just as our times of darkness and hell-visitings are specially our own, and the heart-piercing sword of fire comes as a touching of our deepest centre that is immeasurably special and precious – and personal.

This does not mean we can, so to speak, afford to ignore Teresa's visions. On the contrary, it is by coming into contact with her ardent spirit, and her exalted yet familiar visions of the presences and Presence that surrounds us always and everywhere that we learn to lose ourselves in order to find ourselves. All this is wonderfully expressed by that gentle seventeenth-century poet Richard Crashaw in his poem 'The Flaming Heart', from which we may quote the concluding lines:

> O thou undaunted daughter of desires!
> By all thy dower of lights and fires;
> By all the eagle in thee, all the dove;
> By all thy lives and deaths of love;
> By thy large draughts of intellectual day,
> And by thy thirsts of love more large than they;
> By all thy brim-filled bowls of fierce desire,
> And by thy last morning's draughts of liquid fire;
> By the full kingdom of that final kiss
> That seized thy parting soul, and sealed thee His;
> By all the Heavens thou hast in Him
> (Fair sister of the Seraphim!);

By all of Him we have in thee;
Leave nothing of myself in me.
Let me so read thy life, that I
Unto all life of mine may die!

Fair sister of the Seraphim: what a perfect phrase this is, raising human womanhood to the heights and bringing the highest angels down to earth! We are not angels, but men and women, yet through the indwelling Trinity we too are sisters and brothers of the Seraphim. Sister of the Seraphim, Mother of Carmel she was and is. But above all else, then and now and always, Teresa of *Jesus*.

Part II
Darkness and Light:
St John of the Cross

6

THE LIGHT ON THE MOUNTAIN

i. *Nada y Todo*

The first great work of St John of the Cross is called the *Ascent of Mount Carmel*[1] and is based on a central master image of a journey up a mountain. In a sense then it is a manual of mountaineering, showing the best way to reach the top, and the various dangers to be avoided if the climber is not to come to grief on the way. As a Spaniard John would have known much about mountains, but one wonders how much this sixteenth-century monk knew about the great mountains of the world and the great hazards involved in making the various ascent of these mountains. Did he know about Mount Blanc? Probably he did. Did he know about Mount Everest? Had he ever tried to measure in imagination its immensity and inaccessible summit as some of us have tended to do since our youth? Probably not. But one thing is certain. If he did know of Mount Everest and of the intrepid men who have climbed it, or tried to climb it, he would have said that the dangers and difficulties are as nothing compared with those of the spiritual journey to the inaccessible peaks of the Mount of Perfection, called also Mount Carmel in honour of his Carmelite calling and the brown habit of Our Lady of

[1] The basic text used here is the Silverio-Lucinio edition of the works of St John of the Cross (Biblioteca De Autores Cristianos, Madrid, 1955). Both the standard English translations have been consulted, but in all cases of direct quotations I do my own translation.

Mount Carmel which he wore. (His own brethren tried to
deprive him of this habit as he lay dying at the age of forty-
nine in alien Andalusia, a long journey in those days from
Fontiveros in Castile where he was born.)

Once, or perhaps more than once, he made a sketch of
the Mount of Perfection or the Mount of Carmel. It was
the sketch of a path rather than a mountain. The path was
called *Nada*, and the top of the mountain was also called
Nada. And here we meet the first and perhaps the greatest
paradox of our author, for he was a master of paradox and
of that sharp pointed phrase which earned for him the title
of 'my little Seneca' (*Senequita*) from St Teresa, his great
soul-friend and co-founder, at least in spirit, of the Order
of Discalced or Reformed Carmelites.

Let us look at this first great paradox which governs the
whole strategy of the spiritual journey to the summit of the
mountain. *Nada* means for John both nothing (its literal
meaning) and everything, for it denotes precisely that space
into which everything, that is to say the Divine Infinity, can
flow. *Nada y Todo*: nothing and everything: that is the
whole story of the *Ascent*, at once dramatic, dangerous,
complex and entirely simple. *Nada y Todo*: to make space
for the totality no single, separate, special thing can be
possessed. If we hold only one thing as a possession then
we in turn are possessed by what we hold. This, as John
puts it, 'causes heaviness and weariness of spirit'. But above
all it excludes the Divine inflowing of light and love. So it is
that every particular good, everything that could be held as
a particular possession, must come under the sign of the
Nada, must be radically relinquished.

So we come to those aphorisms or rules of behaviour,
which conclude and sum up John's ascetical doctrine, in
Chapter 13 of the first book of the *Ascent*: indeed these
rules were appended by John to the little sketch or map of

the journey upwards which he used to give to his spiritual
pupils.

> Let your inclinations lie
> Always towards the harder thing;
> Choose the ways that bring not joy
> But the most unpleasant thing.
> For to pass from all to all
> Thou must seek no thing at all.

Nobody has ever read this chapter with serious intent who
has not felt sharp knives pierce their spirit; the words have
sometimes induced a kind of depression, and a despair of
ever managing even the first step of the journey; taken
literally and over-seriously they have undoubtedly contri-
buted to strain and tension and perhaps even breakdown in
anxious and eager youth. More earthy and everyday types
have simply closed the book at this point and said: 'This is
not for me; I must find another way upwards or forever
remain in the foothills.'

We know that St Thérèse of Lisieux studied John's
writings for two full years and found constant nourishment
therein. All the same, it is hard to escape the impression
that her famous discovery of the 'Little Way', as she called
it, was the result of her encounter with these maxims and
this way of tackling the Mount of Perfection. What
Thérèse found in fact was that Scripture seemed to speak
directly and simply to her heart as an invitation to
complete trust and self-surrender. She did not want to say
that this little way was for everybody, but it was the only
way for 'little souls' such as she. As she deepened her grasp
of this new way she felt that it was a way in which many
could follow her, having closed the great tomes of spiritual
direction. In all this she does not mention John even once,
but we may feel certain that she had passages such as *Ascent*

I.13 in mind when she sought in anguish for another path. No doubt she would have felt that when all was said and done her Little Way was no different from the way mapped out by John, but it was undoubtedly more immediately accessible.

It would be unfair both to John and Thérèse to try to smooth out the rough surfaces of their disagreement. Indeed we may venture to say that this whole area of John's doctrine needs to be balanced by what may be called the Carmelite-Feminine. John's way is the way of the masculine as it looks to the mountain tops and traces a sheer and clear line upwards. The way of a woman is to look to the next step and the next resting-place for weary limbs. In practice John was most considerate and tender in his dealings with aspiring youth and enfeebled old age, but he did keep his eyes always fixed on the light on the summit of the mountain. He was at once sensitive and uncompromising. And like every true spiritual guide there was in him something relentless and inflexible, something that would be intolerable were it not being constantly dissolved in tears. Not that John ever quite realised how much he needed his tears.

What John has to say about detachment from the world is in no way original, nor is the absoluteness of his precepts in any way unusual. It will be found variously stated in all the great spiritual guides or founders. Indeed it is already there quite explicitly in the words of Jesus, in that sheaf of counsels sometimes called the 'hard sayings' summarised by the admonition 'He that seeks to save his life shall lose it, and he that is willing to lose his life shall save it'. If we reflect that 'life' or 'soul' in these sayings stands for all that man holds dear then we shall have to admit John's claim that he is doing nothing more than restating the Gospel of Christ.

There is indeed room for a distinction between the harshly ascetical type of religious leader and teacher and those who lead by way of what the *Cloud of Unknowing* calls 'the drawing of that love and the voice of that calling'. Yet the moment we have made this distinction we find that both John and Jesus Himself belong to the gentler side of the distinction. On the harsher side stands John the Baptist and not a few of the Fathers and spiritual writers: perhaps Ignatius stands there, or at least the Ignatian tradition in some of its forms. Certainly some of John's early companions adopted the harsher way, as it seems did John himself in the early days of the reform.

It would appear that in the case of John and Ignatius and many others, including St Patrick as he reveals himself in his *Confession*, there is need to distinguish or set apart an ascetical phase which was a kind of spiritual commando training. This training relaxed its intensity when it had done its work, only to yield place to more interior and challenging trials and testings without, however, disappearing as an essential temper and quality of the will and affectivity. And it would seem that these daunting precepts placed here at the first stage of the mountain journey are to be taken as principles of training rather than principles of everyday living.

'To seek always not the easiest but the most difficult', for instance, would if taken as a principle of life lead to the most patent absurdities, so that, for instance, it would be necessary to write this book standing up using a scratchy pen or blunt pencil and odd scraps of paper. On the other hand if one is undergoing a course of training to prepare oneself for difficult situations of quite another kind, then such a way of acting would be quite reasonable. But the training should run its course, and this kind of attitude should show itself in our strength of mind and will in facing the journey ahead. Much harm has been done in religious institutes and communities, as also in the drawing up of rules and constitutions, by the confusion of principles of training with principles of living. Perhaps in the present instance John himself was partly responsible for this. We do know, however, that, when this point became an issue between Doria and Gracian after the death of St Teresa, John took the side of the gentler approach of Gracian, an approach which nevertheless made little headway in the Carmelite Order until very recent times, when it sometimes became confused with a kind of softness and slackness of which John would certainly not have approved.

ii. *Eros and Agapé*

In the matter of detachment from the goods of earth John is sharp and clear but not particularly original. Where he is truly original is in his uniquely strong emphasis on detachment from heavenly goods, from such things as visions and prophecies and inner assurances by way of illumination or locutions. We know that St Teresa lived fairly constantly in a rich inner world of what she called imaginary and intellectual visions, and we know that John himself was no stranger to this world especially in its auditory side, where he is careful to distinguish several kinds of locutions or words heard interiorly. He does not despise nor reject such heavenly helps, but here at the foot of the mountain as he looks upwards to sheer precipices and shining pinnacles he insists that this kind of baggage has to be completely relinquished. Here too his banner reads *Nada y Todo*. Indeed he spends more time and energy on this mode of detachment than on the more usual one. One reason for this is that he is writing for dedicated men and women, who have left the world behind, the world that is to say as ruled by materialist and sensual values. What he realises is that the affectivity which has achieved this basic liberation may latch on all the more clingingly and desperately to the bright lights and beautiful objects of the new world that has opened up. What John sees with unexampled clarity is that this way of attachment to a higher realm of goods is just as truly a closing out of God as is the grosser attachment to the world of material goods.

However, a formidable ambiguity begins to trouble the reader as soon as he or she realises that what one is seeking at the end of the ascent is itself a heavenly light and the radiance of the heavenly countenance. Surely this is the summit of human joy, the consummation of the marriage of the creature and the Creator. Let us say that in the description dear to Elizabeth of the Trinity it is the meeting of she who is not with He who is, than which nothing can be more deeply and completely joyful. In practice there is a real emotional difficulty in responding to the images of joy and delight in the *Spiritual Canticle* and the *Living Flame of Love* while keeping in mind the massive emphasis on detachment from the spiritual goods and joys that is the central theme of the ascetical doctrine of the *Ascent of Mount Carmel*.

One can dismiss this difficulty by saying that the light on the mountain and the life to be lived on the mountain is of a rare and rarefied substance completely out of reach of the affective and emotional faculties of men and women. One might adapt the terminology made famous by Nygren, the Swedish Lutheran theologian, and say that the atmosphere on the mountain is that of *Agapé* so that there is no room or function for the seductive and ambiguous images and voices of *Eros*: in other words the whole emotional sphere is left behind. It is true that John will still use the language of emotion and affectivity, but this is sheer metaphor or symbol and will lead to intolerable confusion if taken literally or near-literally. The joys of the spiritual marriage have absolutely nothing in common with the joys of human marriage, though this latter provides the best metaphor for the former.

We have here a whole set of problems which most spiritual and mystical writers carefully avoid. Such simple dichotomy and clear discontinuity simply will not do as an interpretation of any of the great mystics. Certainly it will not do as a hermeneutical principle in reading St John of the Cross. The more we allow the natural and bridal imagery which forms the fabric of John's poetry to create its proper atmosphere and resonance, the more we are forced to recognise the basic continuity between the human world and the divine, between the flickering lights of the itinerary and the pure light of the mountain-top. What John wants to guard against at all costs is the contraction of the soul to any limited and limiting object. By the soul (*alma*) he means, as St Teresa does, the whole personality as related to its total destiny, as the Bride of the Divine Bridegroom. So it is that his whole doctrine is based on the infinity of the human ego, on its *capacitas Dei*, its *capacitas infiniti*. This capacity must find in God its centering focus, its summit of apprehension, the wholeness of its knowing and loving. A certain focussing and centering power is part of the soul's resources, and this power tends to home in on some object near at hand, some object by which it sinks downwards to the affective level, and thus misses that which alone is capable of fulfilling all its desires.

But once the principle of total centering, of seeing the infinite, is established, then the light which has been received begins to illuminate the whole world of nature and *eros*, no longer, however, an *eros* that is wild and destructive, but *eros* and affectivity as elements in a total harmony. Here John stands in the Platonic tradition, not consciously but unconsciously, though he will use in the last stanza of the *Spiritual Canticle* an image which recalls the two-horse chariot of the *Phaedrus*. It is one of his most daring images and could only have come from the imagination of a great poet. The verse reads:

> 'And the cavalry came down at the sight of the waters'
> ('*La caballeria/a vista de las aguas descendia*'),

and the explanation which our author appends to this verse is one of the most profound and subtle paragraphs in the whole range of Christian mystical writing. He tells us that 'the cavalry signifies the bodily senses exterior and interior' and that at the culmination of the spiritual journey they partake in their own way of the delight of contemplation. This participation is not direct but indirect and comes by a kind of overflowing (*redundantia*) of the spiritual into the physical which brings refreshment and joy to the senses.[2] The world of the senses here is primarily the world of the goods of earth, but it can obviously be extended to refer also to those heavenly goods such as visions and devotional feelings which must be put firmly to one side in the journey upwards under the banner of *Nada y Todo*.

---

[2] Stanza 40. '*Por cierto redundantia del espiritu reciben sensitivamente recreacion y deleite de ellos.*' Peers translates: 'Through a certain overflowing of the spirit they (the sensual faculties) receive in the senses refreshment and delight therefrom'. Kavanagh-Rodriguez translates: 'It (i.e. the sensory part) can, through a certain spiritual overflow, receive sensible refreshment and delight from them (i.e. spiritual goods)'. These translations, which at first sight seem to say the same thing, do in fact say different things. For Peers the refreshment and delight flow into the senses from the spirit and thus remain spiritual; for Kavanagh-Rodriguez there is question of a sensible refreshment and delight, something arising within the senses as a result of the overflowing of the spirit. What does *sensitivamente* mean? It would seem to bear either interpretation.

However, it is one thing to say that the senses, however understood, can share in the overflow of contemplation and the spiritual marriage; it is another to consider the place of the senses, of *eros* and the everyday human passions and emotions in the life that is thus lived in the clear light of the mountain-top. What place is there here for our common human loves, interests, hobbies, delights and diversions? What of irony and humour and all the more salty side of life? What of art and literature? What of song and dance? What of good food, of wine and tobacco in their place and right measure? Does not John leave all this far behind as did the Puritans in the Reformed tradition: indeed a comparison is sometimes made between John of the Cross and John Calvin from this point of view.

In reply it must be said that John was and remained a medieval scholastic of the Salamanca school. This means that he had a keen sense of the value of natural man and natural ethics. He was the heir to that pre-renaissance humanism which accepted both natural law, natural ethics, and the integrity of natural man. The whole ascetical and mystical life of man is based firmly on the grid of the natural virtues, and that grid remains as the framework of any redundance or refulgence that flows or shines downwards from the mountain-top.[3] The mystic who has reached the heights, and is in a sense established in the atmosphere and radiance of that marvellous world with its ever-expanding horizons, can enter for the first time into the ordinary joys of life with full freedom. This freedom is the common atmosphere of all mystical groups in the first glow of the spirit. It was the atmosphere of the first

[3] '*Habla en perspectiva natural, o se mueve en un plano ascetico-mistico? Volvemos a comprobar que no existe el dilema. Son perspectiva mistica y religiosa honde las raices en la alcantando de lleno la estructura natural de la persona humana.*' Federico Ruiz Salvador OCD, *Introduccion A San Juan De La Cruz* (Biblioteca De Autores Cristianos, Madrid, 1968) p. 310.

Christians, of the early Franciscans, of the first Quakers and Methodists. It was the atmosphere of the Carmelites of the Reform in their early days. Alas, this freedom of the children of light does not last long: it soon becomes clouded and compromised, as happened after the death of Teresa and before the death of John. Indeed it was through the misunderstanding of this holy freedom that John was hounded to his death by those who could not discern the light that was in him.

Those who misunderstood John and attacked him did not understand either the nature of the light on the mountain which filled his whole being, nor at what unbelievable cost that light was won. For though at first the summit of the mountain stands sheer and clear, yet it is far away, not only in terms of a long and arduous ascent but because the journey has to descend into many valleys, some of them utterly dark and deep and full of menace and terror, as we shall see in the next chapter.

iii. *Total Death and Total Life*

It may be helpful to round off this chapter by linking the principle of 'redundantia' or 'refulgence' with a well-known passage in T. S. Eliot's *Four Quartets*. It seems to me that the twentieth century has produced two great religious poems in English: Eliot's *Four Quartets* and David Jones' *Anathemata*. They both deal in different ways with human history as a divine presence in absence: through prayer in the *Four Quartets*, through liturgy in *Anathemata*, each faces the challenge of the gathering up of time into what another poet calls 'the artifice of eternity'. Nothing is unimportant; nothing can be lost. In both cases the task is to let go of life without losing its essence and meaning. So it is that Eliot distinguishes 'three attitudes that are easily confused: attachment to self and to things and to persons, detachment from self and from things and from persons, and, growing between them, indifference which resembles the others as death resembles life, being between two lives – unflowering, between the live and the dead nettle'.[4]

Now John would not have understood this third attitude though we in our day understand it only too well. All too easily the world can become grey and dull, and we can enclose ourselves in small comforts and petty rituals. For John the choice lay between the lesser lights all around us and the true light shining from the mountain-top, a light that shone downwards and took into itself all lesser lights, all the loves and interests of natural man now properly harmonised and given a place in the fulness of life here and hereafter. In our time these lesser lights have all gone out, and we have no light at all that can survive the blinding glare of nuclear destruction: we are in a darker world than even Eliot imagined. So we must find the light on the mountain or resign ourselves to total darkness in the end and total greyness in the here and now. One encounters nowadays the admonition: 'think globally or perish': it has become almost a signature tune for writers on comparative religion. Yet global thinking is no more than an academic or pseudo-academic exercise unless it is illuminated by mystical thinking, that is to say by some refulgence of the light from the mountain-top, a light precious beyond pearls and rubies, even when it is only partly and fleetingly encountered. The choice is no longer between two lives, as with Eliot, but between ultimate life and total death.

In this situation we need an affirmation of life stronger than even the nuclear affirmation of total annihilation. It is only in the totality of John's *Nada y Todo* that this is at all

[4] 'The Four Quartets', Section 4 (Little Gidding).

convincing or even available. For the light on the mountain is also the true life, the life that enlightens all our days and ways.

7

THE DARK VALLEYS

i. *A Mysticism of the Dark*

The journey towards the light on the mountain is a journey through the darkness. This is in a sense a clear and plain statement. Yet it could lead to a radical misunderstanding of the way of St John of the Cross. For the light at the summit is not *beyond* the darkness but *within* it. Not only that: the light is in strict proportion to the darkness, so that the lesser light is found within the lesser darkness and the greater light within the greater darkness. To put it another way at the risk of mixing our metaphors: the lesser heights are shrouded in deep darkness while the far-off summit is shrouded in the very deepest darkness. Nor is there any way of finding it, or even approaching it, except by journeying into the dark, and from the dark into deeper darkness. This is one of John's central affirmations, and it places him firmly within a certain tradition of Christian mysticism.

For, though light and darkness are the two poles of all Christian mysticism, perhaps of all genuine mysticism everywhere and at all times, yet it may be said that according to emphasis and atmosphere we can distinguish between mystics of the light and mystics of the dark. St Teresa of Avila is a mystic of the light, in whose writings the dark is recognised rather than affirmed. So, too, is Catherine of Siena and the Lady Julian. So, too, is

St Bernard and St Bonaventure. St John belongs with Eckhart and the author of the *Cloud of Unknowing* as a mystic of the dark; they both stand in the Dionysian tradition of the hiddenness of God, a tradition that has its origin in that mysterious author called Denis the Areopagite, supposedly the disciple of St Paul, but generally regarded by scholars as a Syrian monk of the fifth century.

We must be careful not to confuse this distinction with that already drawn, between harsh and gentle spiritual guides. This latter distinction has to do with *ascesis*, with what may be called the five-finger exercises of spiritual training: it stands within the first of the traditional three ways: purgative, illuminative and unitive, while the distinction between mysticisms of light and mysticisms of darkness arises further on. (It would be a mistake, however, to see these ways as following each other in strict chronology, and an even greater mistake to think that one can ever really get entirely beyond the asceticism of the purgative way. Yet normally the emphasis tends to shift from one to the other, progressing from asceticism to illuminative experiences and from there to the way of union and that infused or passive contemplation where God takes over and floods the soul with abundance of light and fire, first experientially and then as a continuous habitation.)

It is at the second and third stages, the illuminative and the unitive, that we find it useful to distinguish between mysticisms of the light and mysticisms of the dark, placing John squarely on the dark side of the distinction. This expresses itself most vividly and indeed dramatically in John's eulogies of night and darkness. '*O noche amable mas que el alborado*': 'Oh night more precious than the dawn': these words are clear and carefully chosen, and they affirm the value, preciousness, desirability of the night in itself over against the dawn and the daylight. The reason for this is again clearly stated: it is because the light is to be found within the darkness and not beyond it. So it is that the darkness must be welcomed, embraced, and received into the soul. It is only as the soul is flooded with darkness that it encounters the light.

What the darkness does is to take away all vision at a certain level or depth of perception so that another level of perception may emerge. Let us suppose that somebody comes to me and says: 'Teach me to enjoy the world's greatest music', and suppose that my would-be disciple is passionately fond of Wagner. As a teacher, however, I believe that the world's greatest music (let us suppose) is that of Palestrina, though I am of course very far from denying the greatness of Wagner, nor do I fail to enjoy his music. But if I am to lift my disciple to the appreciation of Palestrina I have to black out Wagner and gradually create in my disciple the new ears he or she needs to enjoy Palestrina. When this operation is fully achieved I can give Wagner's music back to the disciple, who will still enjoy it, but will now see or hear its limitations, that vast emptiness which it opens and does not fill.

It is to be hoped that we do not press this metaphor too far by supposing that the main process in all this was to expose the disciple to a Palestrina who at first seemed dull and boring. Indeed the disciple is quite deaf to this music in the sense that his or her whole field of hearing has become a desert. The point is that for John the darkness is precisely the presence of the new light which painfully creates a new vision. This light is the Divine presence or rather a nearer mediation of the Divine presence. T. S. Eliot, who at this point in his *Four Quartets* is deeply indebted to John and the mysticisms of the dark, calls this 'the Darkness of God'.

Obviously there is risk here, total risk. How do we know that our disciple is really capable of enjoying Palestrina? How does *he* or *she* know that we are not simply destroying them as a listener to the harmonies? Our disciple must be able to trust us totally, and we must be able to trust ourselves totally. We are here in the land of hope, human hope (present in all true pedagogy) and divine hope. The two stand or fall together: if we cannot find hope on the earth we shall not find it in the heavens; if we do not find it in the heavens, in the living God, then soon or late our store of human hope will be devoured by the enemies of man. John can travel onwards in the dark, led by his hope in God who is altogether faithful, yet this hope in God is also and in the first place hope in man, hope that there is in man 'an inner sanctuary beyond the curtain' where already God has his dwelling-place.[5] So it is that where the human is despised or seen as totally depraved by the Fall there can be no mysticism. This is perhaps the greatest tragedy of the Reformation in some of its main currents, though by no means in all its manifestations; it is also the tragedy of that strand of contemporary Catholicism which has largely lost its traditional connection with Greek humanism and the perennial philosophy of the Christian schools.

In other words, a mysticism of the dark needs as its support and background a strong humanism such as Greek philosophy has traditionally provided. It is by no means an accident that the theology of Denis the Areopagite, which is the main source of this mysticism, is deeply coloured by Platonism.

---

[5] See Hebrews 6:19. I take the phrase (as quoted) from the New International Version which brings out a nuance in the original usually missed in translation.

ii. *The Nights*

John did not speak of dark valleys but of dark nights: this is the metaphor that shines new-minted and stamped with the head of the Divine Lover in the poem on which his first great treatise is based. Indeed we must never forget that the poem came first and is in no way a summary of the book that explains it. It is there for all to read. It is as much there for us as it was for John. We have exactly the same hermeneutical rights and obligations as the poet himself. This is true of every truly inspired poem, for inspiration is from above. Every true poet when asked to explain his poetry will say: 'The poem is there and speaks for itself, to you, to me, to everyman. I have given you the poem; I would kill it by giving an explanation.' In the sensitive reader's response to the poem there is a living process in which the poem questions the reader and the reader questions the poem, a spiral of understanding which is the very pulse of the spirit. This spiral is sometimes called the hermeneutical circle, but it is not a closed-in vicious circle but a living dialogue. It is thus that true illuminative meditation on Scripture proceeds.

Nevertheless John yielded to the requests of his Carmelite sisters to write an explanation of his poem, thus showing himself no different from other men faced with determined women. No doubt he was in any case chockfull of spiritual doctrine, and felt that this was as good an occasion as any to set down a complete system. But then a strange thing happened. The systematic treatise broke down suddenly in mid-sentence, for the *Ascent* comes to a shuddering stop. He started again, and again the great systematic treatise broke down suddenly, for the *Dark Night* treatise ends in mid-stanza. Subsequently he was able to complete full expositions of two other poems, the *Spiritual Canticle* and the *Living Flame of Love*, but neither of these is a systematic treatise, but are rather reflections, sometimes rather long-ranging, on the stanzas as they come.

It is essential to keep these considerations in mind in looking at the elaboration of the metaphor of the 'Dark Night' in the *Subida-Noche*.[6] Readers of the poem are indeed invited to follow the systematic treatment in the prose, but they must realise that there is a real danger of being led astray by the prose from the living personal encounter with that marvellous inspired moment in which the heavens opened to give us the poem: '*En una noche oscura*'. It is worth the labour of learning Spanish to get the feel of these inspired verses.

But John *did* systematise the poetry of darkness, and in doing so distinguished in the first place between the *dark night of sense* and the *dark night of spirit*, and in the second place between the *active night* and the *passive night*, so that we have in fact four dark nights: the Active Night of Sense is dealt with in Book I of the *Ascent* and is identifiable with the asceticism of the *purgative way*; the Active Night of Spirit is dealt with in Books II and III of the *Ascent* and is identifiable in a general sense with the way of detachment from the goods of heaven, a process that spans the *purgative way* and the *illuminative way*. One should add that these identifications should not be pressed too hard, but they may help to give us our bearings. In any case what is most original in this part of John's doctrine is his emphasis on detachment from the goods of heaven, from visions, spiritual favours, particular images and illuminations: this last is a very controversial area, as we shall see.

Now what the Passive Dark Night in its two levels of Sense and Spirit achieves or seeks to achieve is exactly the

[6] I use the Spanish title to cover the two treatises, the *Ascent of Mount Carmel* and the *Dark Night of the Soul* seen as a unity.

same happy state of detachment and purity as the Active
Nights aim at. But in the Passive Nights God takes over,
and so to speak becomes present in the sense and in the
spirit as mystical darkness. Now the word 'mystical' is
important here. It is not a common word either in John or
in Teresa, but it is the best word we have to translate the
words they used: *contemplacion, sobrenatural, passividad.*
The key term is *passividad*, passivity, though it is usually
used adjectivally. It is only by having a clear notion of
what they meant by passivity and passive contemplation
that we can have any real understanding of the Passive
Nights of Sense and Spirit. And it would appear that most
commentators miss the importance of this concept of the
passive-mystical in their interpretation of the 'Dark Night'.
Part of the difficulty arises from the fact that, whereas the
Passive Night of Sense is closely interwoven with the two
Active Nights which are, so to speak, everyone's business,
it is yet a strictly mystical experience and so, arguably, not
commonly experienced in its fulness. A Teresian way of
saying this is that while many dedicated folk reach the
Second and Third Mansions, relatively few pass the
threshold of the Fourth Mansions.

Now it is easy to identify various quite genuine spiritual
states and experiences as well as ordinary psychological
states such as depression; and it is easy to match these with
some of the descriptions John provides of the journey
through the Passive Nights, and so we can have a situation
of quite intolerable confusion. The truth it would seem is
that most religious folk remain within the ordinary ways of
active prayer and acquired contemplation, within what
Teresa calls the Third Mansions, with perhaps brief
incursions into the further mansions. One can then ask
whether this non-mystical path takes its own course
upwards to the summit, or whether all are called to the

mystical as the only way to the fulness of divine love and total service to humanity. We touch here on the greatest single controversy in the history of spiritual theology, a controversy seemingly settled by Vatican II in favour of the proponents of mysticism for all, *seemingly*, because it is very doubtful whether the Council Fathers were really pronouncing on mystical matters. For this we have to wait for Vatican III, and perhaps the undoing of the seventeenth-century destruction of the great tradition of mystical contemplation.

Passivity is the key then, if we read John rightly, and passivity is something given to the soul, not something reached by any kind of activity. It is well to note that for John and Teresa ordinary meditative and liturgical prayer is a work of Divine grace in man, grace with which man co-operates, though as far as this point is concerned one could equally adopt the Lutheran principle of grace alone, and in this sense say that all prayer is entirely given. But this is not the passivity or givenness about which John speaks: indeed it could be argued that it was because he was frustrated in experiencing this mystical givenness and receptivity that Luther came to his principle of grace alone and faith alone. He was tired of human striving, and something in him stood in the way of the flowing in of the mystical. Or perhaps something of it did flow in in his 'tower experience', something that remains as a holy light at the heart of Lutheranism. Then, of course, he went on to build up his theological system, and the light became clouded by the system. Something prevented John from completing *his* system: perhaps it was precisely the inner demand and dynamism of the mystical marriage. One could perhaps argue that both John and Luther have their own necessary place in the mighty orchestration of Christian consciousness.

Perhaps the best image of the givenness of the mystical is that of the four waters of St Teresa, where the water stands for the glow and power and illuminative splendour of the Divine presence, which can be touched and glimpsed painfully in the ordinary ways of prayer beginning with the early fervours and sweetnesses which have a light and transient quality. This presence of God is greatly sought and deeply longed for in the ordinary ways of prayer, but it comes only painfully and grudgingly as one waters or irrigates the parched earth, until the time comes when the heavens open, the rain falls, and the whole garden of the soul is filled with the lifegiving water of the Divine presence. In this happy state the soul should remain quiet and not revert to its laborious search for God by way of images and considerations and the sheer plod of formal or informal meditation. The liturgy of the Eucharist and the Divine Office is given new and marvellous life through this experience, yet there is a sense in which the soul in this state is independent of these mediations of grace, and seeks above all else solitude and the inner space to open wide to this marvellous inundation of light and fire.

But this inflowing of the Spirit of God has a dark and painful side, and this is precisely the Passive Nights of Sense and Spirit. The Passive Night of Sense places the soul in a great desert, taking away all spiritual savour, all sense of consolation and heavenly companionship. This state is the same as that called by some writers aridity and by others *acedia*. Indeed this state is, so to speak, a commonplace of spiritual writing and spiritual guidance: it is because they have been unable to recognise it or deal with it that some charismatic groups have fallen apart or fallen back into some kind of affective or emotional substitute for spirituality. What is most special and characteristic about John's treatment of this state is that he sees it as strictly mystical, as something given by God, as a flowing-in of God which is creating a new vision and a new savour as the old perceptions are being cauterised. He insists that those who have been brought into this healing darkness, this purifying desert, this deepest 'vale of soul-making', should not be forced back to what he calls meditation. This is a very delicate point, for obviously such exercises as the meditative reading of Scripture or the response to Eucharist and Divine Office are part of the staple diet of Christians seeking Christ and the Father. Yet, John seems to say, it must be all in the mode of waiting rather than the mode of doing. All doing will achieve is to jog the hand of the Divine surgeon, or more exactly shift the patient's body under his hand with perhaps disastrous results.

Reading John's fulminations against spiritual 'blacksmiths' (in the *Living Flame*) one cannot help wondering whether his passionate warnings have any relevance to our time and place. Do we accord this aspect of his doctrine no more than a museum interest? Hardly. Anybody who has anything to do with spiritual direction, or as we may prefer to call it 'soul-friendship' (translating the Celtic term '*anam-cara*'), hears again and again the plaint or complaint 'I cannot pray'. Usually this goes with distractions and every kind of mind-wandering, or perhaps the upsurge of new or old desires, which is especially heavy when there is some kind of personal relationship going well or ill, or there are business worries, or the clamour of competing commitments.

Now it is easy, in meeting this kind of situation in oneself or in others, to fall into that same activism against which John speaks with such unwonted passion. The tendency nowadays is to say: go out to the poor and lonely and help them, or join the Campaign for Nuclear Disarmament and help save the planet. Or else one talks of the latest spiritual book or course of lectures. Or one takes on some technique of meditation and buys an encephalograph to sort out one's alpha waves. Obviously all these things are good in themselves, especially the first: the kind of spirituality that is not deeply concerned with the poor and lonely is no spirituality at all. But this is not the point. It is prayer that is in question, the relationship of man to the source of his being, and it may be that what is happening in the spirit is a very real and deep encounter with the living God, an encounter through which (as John saw it) more is wrought for the world's welfare than in a thousand works of mercy or service.[7]

iii. *The Passive Night of Spirit*
Before finishing this chapter we must look closely at the Passive Night of Spirit, though for most of us it lies far beyond our present experience, at least in its fulness. All the same, we do all or most of us have glimpses of it, and there are situations of total panic or despair or suffocating horror where its shadow strikes across many ordinary lives. Indeed it may be said that there is a real connection between certain forms of depression and the heights or depths of mystical experience.[8]

We find this best expressed perhaps in the life and writings of Jean-Joseph Surin, who was connected with the events in a French convent made famous by Aldous Huxley's book *The Devils of Loudon* (1952). We are here in a world where only a fool will tread other than warily, a

[7] *Living Flame* I.3.
[8] cf., Fr. Marie-Eugéne OCD *I Am A Daughter of the Church*, tr. M. Verdaclare, (The Mercier Press, Cork, Ireland, 1955). The section in this second volume of Fr. Marie-Eugene's two-volume compendium of Carmelite spirituality (Vol I is called *I Want To See God*) which deals with what the author calls 'psychical phenomena' is surely one of the most helpful things ever written on mental disturbance and insanity.

world where truly angels fear to tread. It is also the world of disease and torture, of the breaking of the body and sometimes of the spirit, of those unknown heroes to one or other of whom we, under God, may owe our inner life in the solidarity of the cross, in what Charles Williams calls the 'co-inherence of sacrifice'.

But to return to the Passive Night of Spirit. It is, John tells us, terrible beyond description, so that no one can endure it for long. Concerning its essential terror he seems to make quite contrary statements: that it is an encounter with Satan and an encounter with the divine purity. Yet here especially Satan, for all his destructive and annihilating power, is the servant of God's purposes. We are in fact in the world of the *Peirasmos* which is, so to speak, the centre of the battle between good and evil. In his great Father-prayer Jesus teaches us to ask the Father not to lead us into the *Peirasmos*, the test, the final temptation. This he had to face himself in Gethsemane, and it almost unmanned him, the Son of Man. It is the archetypal situation of the Book of Jonah when the human self is buried alive in the depths of the dark waters, alone and cast off for ever from all light and peace. Indeed John uses this same Book of Jonah to describe this final dark night of total undoing. All that is left is the prayer of Gethsemane, the prayer of Jonah or of the Psalmist calling from the depths. It is in this prayer that the most totally passive mystical experience becomes the soul's highest activity. It is here most of all that the mystic becomes another saviour bringing light to us all in our deepest fears and travails. It is here most of all that the inner spiritual pollution of our planet is cleansed through springs of living water, springs whose ultimate source is Calvary. One might say that every mystic in his time and place is renewing, unblocking the fountains of salvation. Moreover, it is the inner pollution and the inner aggression

and cruelty in the heart of man that constitutes the real
threat to our survival of which our polluted physical
environment and all the madness of our nuclear arsenals is
but an exteriorisation. War is no more an evil than is a
disease of the skin: it is merely the expression of the poison
within, and in this sense a sign of health, however
overladen by disease. This at least is the central social and
political assertion of Carmelite spirituality as represented
by John. The mystic prays that his brothers and sisters may
have life here and hereafter.

From this Carmelite mystical viewpoint the woman who
joins the protest at Greenham Common or elsewhere may
indeed be doing something significant but may not be
tackling the evil at its source in the spirit-world, which is
the stage on which the drama of human history is being
enacted. The woman or man who penetrates into the
depths of the Passive Night of Spirit is contending with the
nuclear dragon in its deep dark lair in the spirit-world
which is also the heart-world. It was for such women that
John wrote his manual of training, the 'Subida-Noche' and
it is to such women (and such men, if they can be found)
that this manual is addressed today as always. It must not
be forgotten that not all of these women were cloistered
Carmelites. Some were married; some were widows; some
had charge of large households. But all were dedicated, and
this call to dedication is as urgent now as then, more urgent
perhaps.

At the personal level the Passive Night of Spirit marks
the journey across the threshold from particular selfhood
to universal selfhood, not the destruction of self but its
fulfilment in total self-giving, not the loss of personality
but its divinisation. Yet one cannot pass this threshold by
one's own will. It is necessary to be carried as the bride is
carried across the threshold of her new home, for her

father's house is too much loved to leave it, and all the simple and sweet memories of girlhood cling to her heart and mind. For the human bride the hope is that a great new life opens up, and this hope is never altogether fulfilled. But for the Bride of God there is total and everlasting fulfilment: fulfilment not only beyond death but even in this life. Such is the final paradox of the Night that is 'more desirable than the dawn'.

8

THE FIRE IN THE HEART

i. *The Primacy of Love over Knowledge*

It is clear from the previous chapter that for John of the Cross the spiritual path is shrouded in darkness, is indeed almost composed of the very stuff of darkness: the traveller steps safely only as he finds stepping-stones of darkness. The light on the mountain is itself hidden in deepest darkness as is the mountain itself. The whole journey is made in the night, a night without companionship. If lights appear they are false and to be feared: indeed the darkness is accentuated by the presence of a whole army of will o' the wisps. It is true that some illuminations may be acceptable, and may show us some part of the way onwards and upwards, yet they are more concessions to our weakness than real illuminations, allowing us to take a detour where it is not possible for us to take the direct route of the person who travels more quickly and more safely in total darkness.

This is indeed a mysticism of the dark as against the mysticism of the light of a St Bernard or a St Teresa. Yet, as we have noted, this darkness is itself light, a light that is producing new eyes to receive it. It is not so much that 'the dark is light enough' in Christopher Fry's sense, nor yet that we see in a glass darkly in St Paul's sense, though of course John will accept and acknowledge this Pauline obscurity when there is question of the doctrinal form of faith. But the journey towards the fullness of contemplation is made through the dark side of the mirror, so to speak, for this darkness is precisely the darkness of God, the God of Light and Fire, the God who dwells in inaccessible light and is yet palpably and powerfully a consuming fire.

This brings us to the very central and all-pervading principle of John's mysticism, indeed of all true mysticism of darkness as of all negative theology, so-called. The principle is simply this: that the fire in the heart is the eye of the mind. This is clear not only in the *Living Flame of Love*, poem and commentary, where we are at or near journey's end, but also and primarily in the poem on which the *Subida-Noche* commentary is based. What is true, of course, is that the commentary does not get beyond the first two stanzas, both of which deal with darkness, are indeed a kind of eulogy of darkness, which is taken up again in the fifth stanza, taken up, however, in a new mode as it follows on stanzas three and four, which are concerned precisely with the fire in the heart. Even in translation one is able to catch that new mode or mood in stanza five as of a kind of radiation or incandescence which deepens as the poem moves towards its incredibly tender and utterly timeless conclusion.

The '*Noche*' part of the *Subida-Noche* commentary does in fact reach the third stanza. Its concluding unfinished chapter (II.25) begins by setting down this third stanza, and adding a few brief general remarks before embarking on a line by line exegesis which was never written.

The third stanza runs as follows:

> *En la Noche dichosa*
> *En secreto, que nadie me veia*
> *Ni yo miraba cosa*
> *Sin otra luz ni guia*
> *Sino la que en el corazon ardia.*

O happy Night, O secret Night!
Alone and lost to human sight,
Unseeing, I safely, swiftly go,
Led by heart's fire, lit by heart's glow.

At the conclusion of the general remarks or *declaración*
John sets down the first line '*en una Noche dichosa*' and
simply stops. One ancient manuscript says that the treatise
was broken off by John's death; which would place these
tremendously powerful chapters of the second book of the
Noche at the very culmination of his mystical doctrine. But
most scholars give an earlier date to the *Noche* and place it
with the *Subida* in the period 1582 to 1585, that is to say six
years before John's death. It is even suggested that he did
finish the *Noche* and that the rest of the commentary has
been lost. In any case John deals with the more positive and
glowing side of his doctrine in the *Spiritual Canticle* and
the *Living Flame of Love*. However, the *declaración* does
deal summarily with the theme of the light of the heart and
what is said is at once extremely significant and extremely
clear. Here it is:

> Although the soul is not supported on its journey by any light of
> understanding nor by any external guide ... yet is it guided
> onwards by love alone which at this time burns in the heart as the
> Divine Lover calls it onwards, so that it flies towards this same
> Divine Lover without quite knowing how or in what manner this
> happens.

In other words the darkness extinguishes the light but it
does not extinguish the fire, and this fire becomes in fact
the light of the soul by which it is safely guided.

In this passage John places himself fairly and squarely in
a certain philosophical and theological tradition, the
Franciscan tradition of St Bonaventure and the Cistercian
tradition of St Bernard of Clairvaux. It is the tradition
which places love before knowledge, and will before

intellect. It must be noted carefully that the word 'before' has here a temporal as well as an evaluative sense. St Thomas Aquinas, the great exponent of the opposing tradition, will also place love before knowledge in the evaluative sense, thus echoing St Paul's dictum that the greatest of all human dispositions is love (*agapé*). John (and the tradition he represents) here goes further than this in making the light of love a guiding and illuminating principle. He rejects, at least implicitly, the axiom *nil volitum nisi praecognitum* which may be translated: 'you can love only what you know and to the extent that you know it' or better 'whom you know and to the extent you know him or her'. In other words the will cannot or should not push the intellect one step further than the intellect sees. More prosaically, one could say that the heart should not rule the head.

What John seems to be saying here is that the heart does rule the head, and provides a substitute for an intellectual vision that has been totally darkened. It is not surprising that some of John's contemporaries were shocked by this doctrine: indeed this attitude continued even after John's Beatification in 1675. Felix de Alamin writing in 1704 puts this reaction strongly: 'Surely we have here a heresy to beat all heresies, a doctrine that reduces man to the status of the irrational beast of the field, and puts as naught all the lights and revelations of holy men and women.'[9] And in fact it must be admitted that many people have at all times followed the way of blind will and the enamoured heart to destruction, of themselves and/or of others. It is the classical error of the religious leader who batters down all opposition in the name of some narrow enthusiasm. And

[9] *Apud* Federico Ruiz Salvador, *Introduccion A San Juan De La Cruz* (Biblioteca De Autores Cristianos, Madrid, 1968) p. 572, taken from an article in *Ephemerides Carmeliticae*, 1962 (13) p. 461.

indeed some such leaders in our own day have succeeded in turning their brainwashed and broken followers into dumb oxen and shorn sheep. Without going as far as this, some superiors and leaders of communities have demanded blind faith and blind obedience.

But to return to John and this light that burns in the heart. It must be noted carefully that this light is mediated by an accepted doctrine of God, and is felt in the heart as the invitation of God as already known. We are in a world of darkness, but it is, through and through, the darkness of God. In this knowledge God is, so to speak, released from all particular representations and known through what John terms *noticia general y amorosa*, a knowledge at once loving and general. Now the really crucial point here is that the whole world of doctrine, the systematisation of Scripture and Apostolic Tradition known as dogmatic theology, is taken for granted, as also is the whole complex of moral and intellectual virtue. It is above this, resting on it as its foundation and never aside from it, that this general loving knowledge is apprehended. Moreover, there is question of a spirit already kindled and aflame with love, precisely because it has known and meditated the glory of the Lord and His goodness and beauty. It is at this point and from here that the fire kindled in the heart leads the understanding securely forward in the night of all particular knowledge and all special intellectual illumination.

But John is so intent on describing this marvellous process of transformation, this miracle of divinisation forged in the darkness, that he has nothing to say about a process that must normally accompany this process of unitive transformation, the process of growth in holy wisdom, *hagia sophia, divina sapientia*. His poetry is a supreme artistic expression of this holy wisdom. It is true that his commentaries lack the liveliness and freshness of the writing of St Teresa, who for her part had little success with versification. It must also be granted that he had nothing of that salty wit and irony that sparkles in Teresa's letters. Indeed it is significant that John speaks of the heaviness of his own prose style, for this is the kind of judgment only a man conscious of what may be called the rights of the written word could make. For all that, his prose has its own special clarity and power, and rises at times to eloquence and beauty. All true wisdom seeks that beauty of expression which is one of the glories of human intelligence. It must be said then that the fire in the heart is in no way a substitute for insight and understanding at the level of the mind, but rather glows and flashes through the vesture of significant form. More than any other writer St John of the Cross validates Bergson's dictum that the mystic rewrites philosophical and theological discourse in letters of fire.

ii. *Mystical Listening*

The mystical world of St Teresa of Avila was a world of seeing, a visionary world. She was a being of seeing; she drank in the light; she spoke again and again of imaginary visions and intellectual visions. It is true that she was also a listener and experienced what are called locutions or inner speech, but she was not primarily a being of hearing and listening. John, however, tended to dismiss visions and illuminations, not rejecting their right to have a place in the spiritual journey, but stressing their danger rather than their value. In the case of locutions, on the other hand, he goes into explanations and distinctions, sifting and dis- criminating rather than rejecting. Indeed he sees what he calls substantial locutions as of very great profit.[10] These

[10] *Ascent* II.31.

experiences are mystical in the sense of being given and received, and they are authentically and safely mystical in the sense that they are as it were imprinted in the very centre or substance of the soul and effect what they signify. Thus the words *fear not* produce at once, and in their very reception, inner peace and courage, just as the words *be thou healed* spoken by Jesus brought immediate healing and health.

There is, however, a deeper hearing than even that which receives such substantial words, though John does not speak of it in his treatment of locutions in the *Ascent*. This is the hearing which responds to the call of the love of God, the bridal soul listening to the voice of the Bridegroom in her innermost heart. The fire in the heart is in fact the glow of this listening, the ardent response to this invitation. In the passage already quoted from the final chapter of the *Subida-Noche* John tells us that the soul is guided onwards in the obscuration of all vision by the love that burns in the heart as the Divine Lover draws it onward. We are here in an inner mystical space, the place of 'the drawing of that love and the voice of that calling' of the *Cloud* and T. S. Eliot, but it is also a human space and open to the analogy of common life and all the various responses and ardours called forth by the voice of one loved or trusted, or both loved and trusted. Which of us has not felt a leap of the heart on hearing a voice at the door or on the telephone? Who has not at some time been kindled and transported by a letter that tells of new-found love and all its promises, hearing the voice of love as we read. These are but analogies, but they do help us to have some measure of that wonderful and spacious dimension of listening in which John's most ardent mystical poetry has its home.

In his third great poem and commentary, the *Living Flame of Love*, the fire in the heart has become a conflagration, so that the poem and, in its less intense way, the commentary, crackle and sparkle and glow from beginning to end like a log fire in a great old-fashioned brazier – indeed John uses this traditional image to describe what is happening as the fire takes hold of the spirit more and more deeply. At the highest point of union the smoke and crackle all clear away and there remains a quiet deep glowing fire from which tongues of flame issue forth, as the Holy Spirit issues from the ascended glory of the Son in the bosom of the Father, and enters the minds, hearts and bodies of those men and women who had persevered in constant prayer together awaiting the first Pentecost.

In fact the living flame that is the spirit's response to the Divine Lover is simply and profoundly the Holy Spirit. John is quite clear about this, and he begins his commentary by quoting that marvellous text from Romans 8 in which the Holy Spirit is seen as speaking, or rather moving, within the human spirit. 'For we do not really know what to say to God but the Spirit speaks within us with inarticulate sighings'. The Spirit is fire in the heart, and the fire in the heart is the Spirit: so it is that the priest at Pentecost used red vestments, not white or gold as on other great feasts. John produces a rich and rare store of images to express the marvel of this fire in the heart in its flaming fulness. He speaks of kindlings of ever deeper inwardness, yet with it the outwardness of a great fragrance 'as of all the perfumes of the world shaken together'. He speaks of lamps of fire illumining the deep caverns of the heart until one has the sense of each human spirit as a new heavens and a new earth, or of seas or sunset fire like the 'lit sea beneath' of Shelley's ardent sunset in 'The Cloud'. Indeed, the mention of Shelley may remind us that John is the most romantic of poets and indeed called some of his poems romances. It is, however, a romanticism held in balance by the purifying asceticism of the Dark Nights of Sense and Spirit.

The Holy Spirit who is the living flame of love, or more exactly the flame of living love (*llama de amor viva*), is for John also the Spirit of truth, and therefore the best of all guides in the soul's unending journey. He does not develop this aspect of his theology in set terms, yet it is all there in that central powerful and simple image of the lamps of fire (*lampares de fuego*), and it is well to listen for a moment to that third of the four stanzas of the *Living Flame*:

> O *lampares de fuego,*
> *En cuyos resplendores*
> *Las profundas cavernas del sentido,*
> *Que estaba oscuro y ciego,*
> *Con extranos primores*
> *Calor y luz dan junto a su querido*

> O lamps of Fire
> In whose effulgence
> The deep wide caves
> Of man's indulgence
> Bereft of sight
> Bereft of force
> Give heat and light
> To their Lover-Source

There is a whole theology here in germ and promise, for the lamps of fire are the Divine attributes, the faces of God: goodness, holiness, beauty, loving kindness, glory, mercy and the rest. The list is infinite, as is also the number of the dimensions of the heart of man, what John calls 'the caverns of sense'. We may translate this conception rather freely as 'the deep wide caves of man's indulgence' for *sentido* has this nuance here: it is the sensuality of man that is in question, sensuality cleansed and purified by the Nights of Sense, and now to be named sense rather than

sensuality. So it is that the very depths of man which Freud
and his followers have analysed and sometimes illuminated
are the place, vast and cavernous, into which God's glory
shines. One might say that the white light of God becomes
in these caverns a many-crowned glory and so gives, really
gives, back anew and afresh God's glory to Himself. Again
and again John tells us that this involves *noticia*, knowledge,
the kind of knowledge in which the theologian and the
poet speak together or alternatively, as happens so often in
the Old and the New Testaments.

There is here interchange, *commercium*, a two-way
process of action and interaction. Nothing of nature, of
human sensitivity, is lost in this transforming union. The
link between the world of nature and the world of mystical
flowing that seemed to be entirely severed in the course of
the long Nights of Sense and Spirit is here restored. It has
been claimed that John of the Cross, like John Calvin,
broke with the old theology of the analogy of being, that is
to say the theology that sees a continuity between the
goods of nature, especially human nature, and the goods of
grace and the new life in Christ. There are indeed texts such
as *Ascent* II.3.3, where John quotes 'Faith comes through
hearing' (*Fides ex audito*, Romans 10:27) and explains that
faith blinds all man's natural knowledge to leave room for
what is heard. What is not clear from this particular passage
in the *Ascent* is that hearing for John is itself a transforming
experience, an ever-deepening response of the heart as it is
cleansed by the darkness, a heart that includes all man's
desires and needs, all his inner dimensions of longing and
loneliness, joy and pathos, hope and fear (for the fear of the
Lord as a sense of awe and reverence is at the very ground
of this experience). So nature returns, bringing its own
dowry to the mystical marriage of lover and beloved.

iii. *Mystical Humanism*

Undoubtedly one of the most exciting events in religious publishing of recent years is the appearance of an English translation of *Herrlichkeit* by Hans Urs Von Balthasar, the celebrated and controversial Swiss theologian who died in 1988. The English translation entitled *The Glory of the Lord*[11] is not easy reading, but it has its own quality of life and the excitement of large horizons, and is indeed the map of an intellectual journey at once arduous and exhilarating. It is the same journey as that in which John engages us, and indeed it is the necessary complement of John's manual of training and climbing inasmuch as it looks at the whole wide sweep of the great enterprise of Christian self-understanding in the light of the glory of the Lord.

Von Balthasar's book is subtitled: 'A Theological Aesthetics', and its originality (which like all true originality is a blend of the old and the new) consists in the placing of the concept of beauty at the centre of theological understanding. What makes the book especially relevant to our present meditation on St John of the Cross is that Von Balthasar puts at the head of his whole work a text from the commentary on the stanza with which we have been concerned, the stanza concerning the Lamps of Fire.

We have noted that John sees the Divine attributes reflected in the deeps of man's heart so that in a marvellous way these deeps give warmth and light to the Divine Lover. Each of the glories or attributes of God casts, as it were, a luminous shadow over the soul, and this shadow becomes itself a glory: goodness, truth, mercy, strength: all are given back to the source as *new* and living glories. So it is that the Divine Beauty overshadows the soul, and this shadow becomes beauty in the human personality, and so

[11] (T. & T. Clark, Edinburgh, 1982–).

to speak gladdens the eyes of God. So John can write: 'the shadow of the lamp of God's beauty in the soul becomes another beauty to the measure and form of God's own beauty', and it is these words that Von Balthasar uses at the head of his book.

The great question here is the relationship of the beauty of nature and man's own natural being to this Divine Beauty that is revealed in God's self-disclosure in the Scriptures. Do we need new eyes to see the glory of the Lord, or is it rather that this light purifies and strengthens our innate response to the beautiful, as happens also in the case of the true and the good? Does the truth and goodness of God as it breaks into human consciousness simply break to pieces all man's natural conceptions, as Luther thought and, after him, Kierkegaard and Barth? And what of beauty? To what serves mortal beauty? asks Gerard Manley Hopkins. Is it a trap, or is it a doorway to the Divine Beauty? This kind of question is never far away in Von Balthasar's book, and he seems to give different answers to it at different times. As an admirer of Barth, Von Balthasar tends to play down or even reject the continuity between nature and grace, as a follower of St Thomas Aquinas he tends to accept the analogy of being which is an acceptance of continuity: in this mood he sometimes criticises John for his seeming rejection of the world of the senses (Vol. I, pp. 410, 411).

Perhaps if Von Balthasar had looked more closely at the passage he puts at the head of his book he would have seen that John values above all else the world of human feelings and sense perception. What is true is that he is relentless in his demand that this world should be thoroughly and totally purified of possessiveness and narrowing self-indulgence. But it is this region that, thus purified and filled with God's glory, gives not only light but also warmth to the Beloved. This warmth is always a human warmth, full of tears and pathos as well as sweetness and harmony, full of that special fragrance that comes from the breaking of the jar of precious ointment that was the heart of the woman who came to the feet of Christ.

A great loneliness and despair descended on Western European man in the late Middle Ages as men ceased to feel themselves overshadowed by the Divine presence in the world of thought. John was an heir to this loneliness and despair, as was Luther, as was Descartes later on. In the face of this despair Luther latched on to Christ in total faith, and in doing so left man's humanity in the outer darkness, in itself utterly lost, redeemed only in the sense of being covered over by the grace from above. This is also the view of Barth, and to some extent of Von Balthasar. It is the shadow of Augustine that lies across all Western theology apart from Celtic theology, or rather the shadow of the dark side of Augustine. It seems at first sight that John lies as deeply in this shadow as did Luther and Calvin. But the more deeply one reflects on a text such as that concerning the lamps of fire the more one sees that John, for all his asceticism and harsh disciplining of natural appetites and tendencies, sees man as basically good, sees human nature as waiting not to be covered over by the cloak of grace but rather waiting to be fulfilled and illuminated in all its natural powers and possibilities. In other words John is a Christian humanist, not, however, stopping short at the humanism of Erasmus but going on to a mystical humanism in which the Fire in the Heart becomes the presence of the Divine Beauty and Goodness in the soul of man.

9

THE FOUR SPIRITS

i. *Divine Motherhood*

The *Dark Night of the Soul* of St John of the Cross is one of the peaks of Christian mystical writing. It is a twin peak and must be seen balanced by the *Ascent of Mount Carmel* as the mountain where I was born near Killarney is balanced by its sister mountain, so that both together are called the Paps of Dana. The comparison is not entirely fanciful or irrelevant, for the image of two rugged peaks that assume the shape of the most consoling image of childhood does indeed say something essential about the right approach to these twin treatises that seem at first reading, or even after many readings, harsh and even frightening, and yet may come to be cherished as fountains of special, indeed unique, consolation and manifestation. It is not without a certain artistic intention that St John brings forward the image of the Mother-God in the first book of the *Dark Night*, and centres all he has to say around it. It is all about the soul being weaned from the breasts of Divine consolation, and he uses a rather intriguing item of ancient mother-wit to make his point. Apparently the Spanish mothers of his day used that bitterest of substances, aloes, to discourage their babies from holding on to mother's milk too long – no wonder they produced mystics and conquistadores! But motherhood does not cease with weaning, and it is well to keep this image of a mothering

God with us as we try to scale the dizzy heights of the *Subida-Noche*, where 'the way up and the way down are the one way'.

In what follows we shall be concerned with the *Dark Night* only and with one aspect or approach to it, but our analysis has to be seen in the context of this image or idea of the motherhood of God, which we will return to at the end of the chapter with a conclusion that might otherwise seem unfounded if not totally unacceptable.

ii. *Man and God*

The treatise on the Dark Night of the Soul falls into two parts: Book I deals with the Night of Sense, Book II with the Night of Spirit. As we reach the later chapters of Book I, however, it becomes clear that there is really one night, the Night of Spirit and that the other night is essentially a preparation for it, even though only the strong and chosen few go the whole way (I.11.4). This is not to say that the material world and the world of desires and emotions (where the first Dark Night operates) is ignored or devalued by our author: indeed for him it partakes in its own way of the final harmony and glory, as is clear from the final stanza of the *Spiritual Canticle*. But (he says) much has been written on this, and little or nothing on the Night of Spirit (I.8.2), so the whole treatise focuses on the Night of the Spirit, and moves towards it as its proper terminus.

Moreover, it is the Night of Spirit that centres that imaginative and dramatic tension which lies always close to the surface in John's writing: this is the artist in him breaking through the scholastic and pedagogical frame-work of his prose. As the treatise opens out in Book II we find that what is being described is a communication and confrontation of spirits. There is the spirit of man which, as

John asserts several times, forms the one *suppositum* or substance with the sensual and bodily part of man: John is no more a Cartesian dualist separating spirit and matter as absolutes than he is a monist in the modern mode of the kind that fails to see that this one *suppositum* is immortal. As with Shakespeare, his great contemporary, death involves for him no more nor less than to 'shuffle off this mortal coil' leaving not only spirit but also the 'inner body' or *anima sensitiva* to go onwards to judgment and eternal life or eternal death, to go onwards most probably to *material* purgatorial fires if it has not been thoroughly purified by the spiritual fire of the Night of the Spirit in this life (II.12.1).[12]

There is, secondly, above and beyond, yet intimately present *within*, the spirit of man, the Spirit of God, the Holy Spirit whose presence was first sweet and tender as mother's milk but now in the time of purification is dark and painful beyond description. In John's theology of mystical union, and the journey towards this rare and mighty mystery of divinised humanity, the principle on which everything depends is that the Dark Night is in truth the very light and radiance of the Spirit of God as it takes ever deeper possession of the soul, as fire takes ever deeper possession of the log of wood until the log becomes itself

---

[12] For the philosophical tradition rooted in Platonism, which came to John through the Victorines, the Rhineland Mystics and the great scholastics such as St Thomas and St Bonaventure, the 'soul' which survives death is much more than pure spirit or pure intelligence. Thus for St Thomas the dead body cannot be identified with the living body: they are different entities: the vitalising, animating *anima* goes along with the spirit in the journey beyond death. There is no question of the survival of a 'ghost in the machine'. It is true that the soul awaited resurrection 'in the flesh' after the General Judgment, and that this fitted uneasily into Platonic immortalism, but the thesis of the survival of the *suppositum* (in John's sense) was not put in question.

pure fire.[13] Indeed he does not hesitate to say that the soul thus filled with the Spirit of God becomes as soul (i.e. as *suppositum*) 'more divine than human' (II.13.11). There is even a sense in which the Spirit of God takes over from the human spirit after the manner of a new formative and animating principle (II.8.5). This is the death of the human spirit in order that it should be born again by means of the new form that flows in (II.9.6).

We must be careful here. John is in no way affirming a facile 'born again' theology of the fundamentalist type. For John the rebirth comes from within as the seed 'dies' into its fulfilment. This is a slow and devastating process, literally a living death which passes into new life. However much it is God's work – and the Passive Nights are doubly *given*, by common and special grace – nevertheless it is work done *in* the human spirit and with the human spirit's co-operation. Nobody has more eloquently described the cost of this impossible possibility of rebirth from within than John: indeed his relentless logic needs to be softened by keeping St Teresa near at hand to encourage us to take one step at a time. In principle, however, the two Carmelite doctors are in total agreement, and are indeed both of them totally true to the Christian mystical tradition which is already clearly stated by St Paul. However, Christians both Catholic and Protestant, have found a thousand side-tracks to avoid facing this straight and narrow path to the Holy Mountain and the meeting of the spirit of man with the Spirit of God.

[13] *Dark Night II.*10. This image of the glowing log of wood is common among the medieval mystics and goes back at least as far as Hugh of St Victor in the twelfth century, See *Medieval Mystical Tradition and St John of the Cross* by a Benedictine of Stanbrook (Burns and Oates, London, 1954) p. 29. It is well to remember that John stands in a long and rich tradition not all of it accepted by the magisterium of the Church. John's Beatification (1675), Canonization (1726) and Doctorate of the Church (1926) all represent important steps in the acceptance of the tradition to which he belongs.

Much can be said about this union of the Spirit of God with the human spirit. Much has been said both by St Teresa, emphasising the light-aspect of this encounter, and by St John emphasising the darkness-aspect. These are indeed golden pages, at once transcendent and entirely realistic in which, to use once again Bergson's beautiful image, the affirmations of Christian doctrine are over-written in lettering of fire. Here, dealing with the dark side of the encounter, one can only point to those powerful first ten chapters of Book II of the *Dark Night*, making just two observations.

Firstly, there is the principle, thrice-repeated (II.5.3; II.8.2; II.9.11) that 'the more clear and pure is the supernatural light the more it darkens the soul, and the less clear and pure it is the less it darkens the soul' (II.8.2). At first sight this principle seems to assume that there is nothing but darkness in natural man, and indeed there are phrases and images in John that seem Lutheran in their pessimism. We must, however, place this aspect of John's theology in its philosophical context. John did not reject Greek humanism, as Luther did. Rather does he assume this Christian Hellenism all the way, not only in its Aristotelian/Thomistic stream but also in the Dionysian stream that derives from Plato and Plotinus. In this tradition the human soul is good, and is indeed *capax dei*, even though it lies in the shadow of the Fall and under the constant jeopardy from the very real and very powerful forces of darkness, Satan and his legions. The soul is plunged in darkness precisely because it is already in the light, but this light is a lesser light, and it must yield place to the greater light. Indeed it can be said that it is only by way of the lesser light that the greater light comes to be accepted. Moreover it is one and the same set of faculties: memory, intelligence and will, that receives the light and with it a larger scope of operation. It must be noted especially that the transforming union brightens and deepens the natural intelligence as regards not only heavenly things but earthly things as well (II.8.5). The darkening and debilitation of the intelligence is but a temporary phase which should lead to its fuller and more penetrating use. John has no use for that soggy pseudo-humility which has unmanned some of his followers.

Our second observation concerning this theology of darkness must be brief. It is this. In his demand for total self-giving, in his insistence on the straightness and narrowness of the pathway to the Holy Mountain John is saying nothing that is not laid down clearly in the teaching of Jesus given in the four Gospels; and as Jesus distinguishes, in dealing with the rich young man, between the common way and the path of perfection, so does John. Moreover he sees this path not just in personal but in ecclesial and cosmic terms, as the best if not the only way to share actively in the salvation of the world (*Spiritual Canticle* s.29).

iii. *The Third Spirit*

The spiritual drama which St John of the Cross unfolds with unique power and precision has its centre or axis in the relationship of the Spirit of God to the spirit of man. However, there is here, as in the New Testament, a third *persona dramatis* whose role is in a sense subordinate yet who is demanded by the script, so to speak, and whose presence not only heightens the tension but in a sense creates it. This third spirit appears intermittently all through the treatise and is so conventionally presented that the reader can miss its importance. However, all this changes dramatically in *Dark Night* II.23 where this third spirit seems almost to take over from the Spirit of God as the 'antagonist' of the human spirit.

This third spirit is, of course, Satan, the devil or demon, *el Demonio*. Throughout the treatise *el Demonio* is, with the world and the flesh, one of the three enemies of the soul: here John is doing no more than presenting the traditional cautions and prescriptions, with his characteristic sharpness and clarity. But here in Chapter 23 we come, quite unexpectedly on a passage omitted from some of the early edition of the *Noche*, (pars. 8.9.10) in which *El Demonio* becomes the very darkness of the Dark Night, oppressing the human spirit with disturbance and horror (*turbacion y horror*) which 'causes greater torment to the soul than can come to it from anything else in this life' (par. 9); and this it would seem because there is a naked contact of the evil spirit with the human spirit (*espiritu a espiritu algo desnuda*).[14]

These strong and fearful phrases call to mind the Synoptic accounts of the agony-prayer of Jesus in Gethsemane when 'horror and dismay came over him' as he entered into the hour of the powers of darkness (Mark 14:34 NEB). Yet, strangely, John does not refer to this passage either here or elsewhere in the treatise on the Dark Night.[15] And this reminds us of a curious fact: that John does not at all consider the prayer-experience of Jesus in writing about these exalted matters. Surely it is here especially that the Christian is in the way of the following of Christ? Did not the man Jesus who had to face the

[14] For textual information see the critical apparatus of the Crisogono/Lucinio edition (Biblioteca De Autores Cristianos, Madrid, 1955, *in loco*).

[15] According to the Kavanagh-Rodriguez *Scriptural Index* there is only one reference to the Gethsemane text in the whole of John's writing and this as illustrating a point in connection with vocal prayer. (*Ascent* III.44). There is also a reference to the distress of Jesus in John 12:22–27: See *Spiritual Canticle* s.14/15. par. 10.

assaults of Satan in the Temptations and in Gethsemane
have also to face the trials of the Dark Night of Spirit? But
for John is seems that the union of the Holy Spirit of God
and the human spirit of Jesus is perfect from the beginning.
In relation to the disciple travelling through the darkness
Jesus is indeed the Bridegroom and companion, but only as
the Perfect One totally united to the Father. There is one
point, however, where, for our author, Jesus is not only the
guide who is perfect and perfected, but the guide who is
himself undergoing all the terror and desperation of the
deepest darkness. This is at the point of the *Lamma
Sabacthani*, when 'at the moment of death he was
annihilated in his soul without the least relief or consolation' (*Ascent* II.7.11). However, John is careful to add
segun el parte inferior, according to the lower or sense part
of the soul. This is not, for all its superhuman scope and
terror, the Night of Spirit. This it would seem was not, for
John, a road that Jesus had to travel, though he is at all
times our hidden companion along this straight and narrow
path.

The matter is quite different when there is question of
that naked contact of spirit with spirit described in *Dark
Night* II.23, and which, we are told, is a greater suffering
than any other torment in this life. This experience may be
part of the purification by which the summit of union is
reached, but it may also be encountered *at* the summit and
indeed belongs properly to the world beyond death
(para. 10). It is significant that St Teresa speaks of a similar
confrontation with the Powers of Darkness after the
Seventh Mansions have been entered.[16] It must be noted
carefully, however, that this kind of experience lies outside
the main itinerary of the Dark Nights and may, in some
measure, be given to anyone who enters the spiritual way.

[16] *Interior Castle* VII.2.

We have here two important linkages which one can only mention in passing, linkages between John (and the tradition to which he belongs) and other traditions of Christian devotional theory and practice. One linkage is with the devotion to the Heart of Jesus, especially the practice of the Holy Hour, which is seen as a sharing in the Gethsemane Hour of the Saviour and an entry into his saving work by way of compassionate love. The other devotion is that of the Holy Souls, according to which we share some of the purgatorial experience of those who have died, and so enter more deeply into the Communion of Saints: the assumption here is that we who are in the world of freedom can open doors of grace and glory which are (as such) no longer available to those who are already in the world of the spirits, of evil as well as good spirits. There is also a connection here with the consciousness of the needs of the dying, who may have to face, as Robert Browning says, 'the arch-fiend in his most terrible form'.

None of this is present in John's text, nor does he in fact link this demonic experience with the Gethsemane or Desert experience of Christ: this link is only made at the level of the Active Night and at the lower level, as we have seen. And of course the demonic experience does fit in better at the active level since it is not really part of what God accomplishes directly in the sense or spirit by way of mystical darkness. It does nevertheless issue in spiritual purification, and this we shall look at in the next section which will bring in the fourth order of Spirit involved in the great drama of the Night of the Spirit.

iv. *The Two Undoings*
As befits a mystic in the Dionysian tradition, St John of the Cross assumes the presence of the spiritual hierarchies in the spirit-landscape that he depicts with such grace and

power. Now and then they come forward, especially when, as in our present text, there is question of the demonic world which is the world of fallen hierarchies, the Spirits of wickedness in the high places of which St Paul speaks (Ephesians 6:12): indeed in all his angelology and demonology (as elsewhere) John stays close to the landscape of the Bible as he understands it: an understanding which, on the whole, one would defend against certain of our contemporary schools of exegesis – indeed the tide is turning already today in John's favour.

To return to the present text: Chapter 23 sets out to explain the words 'in darkness and concealment' especially the word 'concealment'. We are told that at a certain stage of union the work of God in the human spirit takes place directly and not, as is ordinarily the case, through the mediation of the angels (II.23.11). Already in Chapter 12 John has stated the general principle of angelic mediation: the Divine light 'descends from God from the first hierarchies unto the last, and from these last unto men' (II.12.3). In this process the angels themselves are purified, and even share this light with each other. Here the modern reader will ask, perhaps impatiently, why this Divine light cannot reach the human spirit directly. John's answer would be that the human spirit is totally incapable of receiving this pure and holy light. No man or woman can see God and live. Jan Ruysbroeks, one of John's sources, speaks of 'the terrible and immense love of God' (*Mirror*, Chapter 17). Indeed the Old and New Testaments are full of this mediation of the Divine mystery, which yet reveals itself directly to certain such people, such as Enoch, Moses and Elijah. Only three of the apostles could ascend to Tabor and descend to Gethsemane, and even they remained outside the bright cloud and the garden darkness. For the doorway to the world of the Lord of Spirits opens not only into the light of God that seems darkness to the human spirit but also to that annihilating darkness by which the spirit of man is in danger of total undoing.

Now what John is saying in this Chapter 23 at the end of Book II of the *Dark Night* is that, until such time as the Divine presence can enter the substance of the purified spirit directly, we are served by the good angels who mediate God's light, and attacked by the demonic spirits who try to destroy us. And he enunciates a principle of balance or equivalence which appears fairly constantly on the mystical tradition. The Devil has, as it were, rights according to a measure of justice (*la proporcion de la justitia*). 'God must allow a certain parity (*paridad*) between the two warriors, the good angel and the bad, in their fight for the human soul' (II.25.6). So it is that the adversary will have a large place in the drama of spiritual growth and transformation. Yet at a certain stage of purification the Spirit of God can reach the human spirit directly and Satan can neither know this nor intervene in the matter. This still leaves open the whole domain of the cosmic warfare in which man can help Christ and the good angels to save his fellowmen, and this is something open to the soul at all levels of development, though it is clear that it is those who have been healed and transformed by the Divine darkness who enter most deeply and terrifyingly into this spiritual combat.

Yet, at this point, the question remains: how is it that the contact of the spirit of man with the Holy Spirit of God causes the same kind of distress to the human spirit as the distress caused by the contact with the dark spirit of annihilation? That this is John's doctrine can be seen by comparing Chapter 6 of Book II, dealing with the effect of the Spirit of God on man, with our present text (II.23.8–11). There is clearly in each case an experience of undoing and even annihilation. It can be said immediately that what God is annihilating is the shell of self-love that encloses the spirit, whereas Satan is striving to annihilate the spirit itself. As far as the soul is concerned the *sense* of undoing and annihilating power may well be the same, just as in the times of consolation the dark spirits may take on the form of an angel of light. Either way one is left searching for a principle of discernment. How can we discern between what destroys selfishness in us and what destroys self in us, between what divinises and what enslaves? We shall face this question in the next section.

v. *Humility*

We know that the *Ascent of Mount Carmel* is a journey towards transforming union, and that the passive Nights of Sense and Spirit are simply the flowing in of the Divine presence until in the fulness of this flowing union is reached. Further, we know that for St John of the Cross this union has an ecclesial and cosmic dimension, so that it is by far the best way of bringing justice, peace and holiness into our world. This is all a well-rounded doctrine for, so to speak, well-rounded persons. Yet such persons are as rare as white blackbirds, as St John freely and fully recognises (I.12.4; II.1.1). This would mean that for the vast majority of Christians, even dutiful and devoted Christians, the treatise on the Nights is irrelevant and best left unread, lest it produce illusions and illusory hopes.

This is not so, however. For John carefully distinguishes a secondary purpose both in the case of the Night of Sense (The Night of Aridity) and in the case of the Night of Spirit (The Night of Undoing). Both Nights serve the great purpose of humility, both for non-contemplatives (I.9.9) and for those who are only partly contemplatives (I.14.5; II.1). If we look carefully at this secondary purpose of the

Nights we begin to see that it is humility that is the key to *all* that the Nights accomplish, and that it is by a fuller understanding of mystical humility that we may be able to distinguish between the distress caused by God (and his angels) in man's spirit, and the distress caused by the evil spirits (and which is allowed by God according to the measure of justice).

Briefly, the Divine presence produces the humility of *life* while the evil spirit strives (and in a sense succeeds) in causing the humility of *death*. The humility of life dissolves our self-conceit, chastens our arrogance, pierces our self-absorption, opens us up in all simplicity and sweetness to others, even to those who wound us and persecute us. In all this our ownmost self, our most secret countenance is being revealed and released painfully, more painfully, most painfully, beyond all reason painfully as our deepest dogmatisms and presuppositions are torn to shreds. This is what I have called elsewhere the way of the third and fourth liberations.[17] This may well be a way of fear and trembling, but it issues in life and creativity.

Far different is the humility which the dark spirit induces. This is the humility of the slave before a master of absolute power and total cruelty. It calls forth a grovelling and conniving servitude, such as indeed the God of some religions and religious experiences seems to demand. It is thus that Satan hides in the best of all hiding-places, the face of God or the face of Christ. It is only the mystic who is truly brought face to face with this demonic God, and thus is able to cleanse his image of God of all vestiges of this masquerade, vestiges such as we find in so many representations of God as total power and invulnerable judgment. We find St Augustine taken in by this false image of God and serving it more and more as he grows

[17] *The Holy Mountain* (Michael Glazier, Wilmington, Delaware, 1983) Ch. 7.

older. We find Michelangelo in his 'Last Judgment' investing the face of Christ with this demonic power. We find many a churchman taking on something of the countenance of this self-righteous and condemnatory God. We all tend to fall into this trap, unless we are chastened and purified by the mystical nights, and brought face to face with this demonic power in its naked annihilating force.

When Jesus was going to meet the Prince of Darkness he said, in the account of the Fourth Evangelist, a strange thing. He said 'the Prince of this world comes, and in me he has not anything' (John 14:30). In other words, there was the total confrontation of spirit and spirit, what our author calls 'the naked contact' of spirit and spirit. For the most part people are insulated from the demon outside by that part of the demonic that is within them. So it happens that it is only when the human spirit is pure, and to the extent that it is pure, that it can meet the dark spirit in all its dark power, in all its annihilating force. Moreover it is this contact with the evil force that pushes the human spirit towards the Divine purity, and towards the fulness of humility as a living, creative and total attitude. It is precisely because the dark spirit asks for abject and slavish adoration (as in the third temptation of Jesus) that we know the truth of our adoration of the Lord our God. Like Elijah we stand before him against all counterfeit service and servitude; like Mary Magdalene we kiss his feet in the sublime boldness of a love that faces mockery and persecution. For humility is endless, as a poet has said, endless and endlessly creative and full of exuberant life.

vi. *The Womb of God*
Finally, to end as we began by recalling John's image of the motherhood of God, one can talk also of the womb of

God, that seems as dark as the darkest night and as enclosing as the belly of the whale. But our God is the God of Mother Earth and Mother Mary. He/She is the God also of the dark womb of Sheol, and there is a recurrent hint in the mystical tradition that Sheol too will in the end serve the great mystery that is hidden in the darkness of God. All we can do is, with all reverence, salute this mystery in passing.

Part III
Cloister and Cosmos: St Thérèse of Lisieux

10

THÉRÈSE MARTIN IN HER TIME
AND PLACE

i. *The House of Dreams*

The place is not hard to find. You take a train north from Paris, an hour's run or so on the very efficient French railway network, the 'iron roads' as they call them. The land is flat and heavily scribed with man's care of it and exploitation of it, more of care and less of exploitation than one finds in most other 'developed' areas. It is a land of beautiful moated houses or chateaux built of mud and wood, for nowhere in these wide flatlands is there a single sizeable stone to be found. Thinking of the place and habitat of that other Teresa, Avila of the Knights, which was also called Avila of the Rocks, one tends to see, perhaps for the first time, some point in the title of Vera Sackville West's book *The Eagle and the Dove*. For indeed this is a land suited to doves and dovecots as Avila is to eagles and inaccessible eyries. But this thought leads to another, perhaps in the end more relevant, the thought that neither the woman of Avila nor the women of Lisieux ever left the place of their early memories, though the Mother of Carmel did indeed travel the length and breadth of Spain, and it can be said that both had equally what may be called the missionary imagination.

Once you are in the town of Lisieux distances are easily manageable on foot, and it is no long walk from Thérése's childhood home *Les Buissonnets* to that other house where

she lived the second part of her short life, about the same
length of time indeed, for she was already a bright and
sensitive five year old when her parents changed their
abode from Alençon to Lisieux in 1877. It is a short
distance from the one house to the other in the fussy
modern town of Lisieux, a shorter distance in the quiet
nineteenth-century town. A short distance, and Thérèse
tripped along lightly from the one to the other in those
days. But in another sense a long distance, a long distance
ever lengthening to infinity. For in leaving *Les Buissonnets*
and entering the convent in the Rue de Carmélites, Thérèse
was passing from the house of dreams to the house of
reality.

Most young women who leave their father's house are in
some measure leaving a house of dreams or rather a house
of dreaming, for of course the dreams have to do with what
lies ahead, with the house of the human bridegroom or the
earthly house of the Divine Bridegroom, a place of the
realisation of beauty, love and holiness. And some women
never quite manage to cope with the first shock of reality.
Fortunately there is usually a time of cushioning, a gradual
awakening from the world of dreams. Yet this is perhaps
the most dangerous factor of all, especially in the world of
the cloister. The eager novice may find a sympathetic
older woman to nourish and sustain her and help her to
awaken gently to the stern world of the cloister. But the
sympathetic older woman may well connive with the
novice's dream world, perhaps in order to possess her as
only such a being can possess another, with infinite
subtlety in the use of all the words and usages of the most
perfect piety. So it is that the house of reality becomes not
simply another house of childhood dreams, a place of
innocence and health, but rather a house of unreality.

Thérèse Martin was marked for possession even by the

very name she received: Thérèse *of the Child Jesus*. Indeed the name was right, but the intention was wrong: she was not only to cherish the childhood of the Word made flesh, but was to be herself always the little one, the baby of the family, the eternal child. Did not Jesus himself say that it is as a little child that one enters his Kingdom? And Thérèse quickly latched on to texts such as 'if any one is little let her come to me', and from there she went on to work out what she called her 'Little Way' the way upwards to the heights of divine union for those she called 'little souls'.

But this littleness was in truth a denial of littleness and of all the pieties of infantilism. For it was a littleness related neither to her sisters nor to her prioress, nor indeed to any human magnitude, feminine or masculine, not even to priest or bishop or pope. It was a littleness directly related to the Most High God, unmediated, independent, utterly beyond question, though not beyond the anguish of the facing of questions. What if Rome had solemnly condemned this way of total trust in the father-love of God? This kind of anguish was spared her in the external order of things though not deep down, where her spirit had to face the infinite and all-encompassing dark. Here we need to note that this option for childhood and littleness cut right across every effort of prioress or elder sister to manoeuvre Thérèse into a mother and child relationship, however much she was willing to use and even develop the language of infantilism. Indeed she could only transcend this intolerable situation and its silken bondage by hiding her independence behind the language of childish dependence. This point is well expressed in one of the best books on Thérèse: *The Hidden Face* by Ida Görres (Burns and Oates, London, 1959). It must be added, however, that not even Ida Görres has been able to describe the full dimensions of a reality that carried Thérèse on and on in the place which, by her own radical and continuous choice, had become the house of reality.

ii. *The House of Reality*

When Thérèse Martin entered Carmel and became Sr Thérèse of the Child Jesus she realised that she was entering a place of bleak austerity and total enclosure. She had no illusions about all this; indeed it formed an essential part of her dream of dedicated virginity, of an affectivity and vitality sacrificed to the Most High God. She was already too good a theologian to see this sacrifice negatively, as a mere denial of the human in the name of a higher ideal. She understood well that this asceticism was simply the condition of growth and transformation, not a way of death but a way of life, of a life lived in the here and now, in beauty, love and holiness. It is important to remember that the Martins were not Jansenists, indeed were if anything anti-Jansenistic in their emphasis on love rather than fear, in their practical belief in frequent communion, in their sense of fun and celebration. Thérèse was a mimic and a born storyteller. Mother Gonzaga, who was as shrewd as she was domineering, called her *une comédienne*, and this salty sparkle appears even in the last pages of her autobiography written in pain and inner darkness, especially in her lively description of her efforts to continue her writing in the face of the fussy goodwill and sheer curiosity of some of her holy companions who passed by as she sat in her chair in the open air.

But what she had to undergo at the physical level went far beyond this sensible and healthy austerity. The convent was cold and damp, and the beds were not only hard and uncomfortable but insufficiently provided with coverings, so that Thérèse simply lay and shivered through the winter nights in times of severe cold. So too in the choir-chapel in which the long meditations and offices were held – up to six hours each day. Thus she suffered day and night in times of cold weather, and so the way was prepared for the breakdown of a strong and healthy young woman who came of durable stock, and whose sisters in the same convent lived to a great age.

This last point cuts both ways, however. For these sisters of Thérèse, all three of them, had to undergo the same icy regime as had the other sisters in the convent. As fas as we know it killed nobody but Thérèse. She was perhaps too young when she was first subjected to it; almost certainly she was among those women who are especially sensitive to cold. But above all she had already accepted her destiny of martyrdom, of special witness to love, of the total following of Christ. So, rightly or wrongly, she did not make her case known, not even when the indications of a physical breakdown were clear to her. She evaded the probings of her aunt Guérin, who seems to have been a sharp and motherly woman, and who was clearly worried about her young niece's pallor and weariness. She went her own way, following her beloved Jesus to Jerusalem, into the Garden, and on to Calvary. There is no defending her treatment of her own body and her response to the solicitude of a much-loved aunt, except on the grounds of a very profound interior call and a deep personal decision unmediated by superior or spiritual director. Make what one can of it, the truth is that Thérèse went her own way, however much she used the language and structure of obedience. In this she was very like Teresa of Avila, who always found a director to agree with her, and then followed his advice with total humility. For both of them the reality that called them on could brook neither refusal nor intermediary. There is here a stubborn wilfulness which can be pierced only by the true cross, or (which is the same thing) by the sword of Simeon. The place of reality is the place of this piercing.

We have noted Thérèse's physical martyrdom, and in a sense this was what she expected and even sought. What she neither expected nor sought was the martyrdom of the heart, first through her father's insanity, especially as reflected in the convent world of continuous reflexion and reaction; then through the gradual realisation that she was the main prize in a power struggle between the formidable Mother Gonzaga and Thérèse's own sister Pauline, Mother Agnes, who alone had the strength to challenge Mother Gonzaga; finally through the realisation that her charity had to work always against the grain, accepting pretentiousness, infantilism, barrenness of heart, sheer and irremediable obtuseness, as if they were the genuine coin of Christian reality, taking all this in without being taken in by it, loving without hope, carrying on from day to day. There were, of course, kindred spirits also and times of laughter and joyful sharing, but Thérèse saw herself as being especially concerned with those psychological and spiritual casualties of which it would seem the Lisieux Carmel had more than its fair share.[1]

It was during the first of her winters in the convent that Thérèse added a second attribution to her name: she was in future to be known as Sr Thérèse of the Child Jesus and of the Holy Face. The Holy Face is the face of Jesus in the

[1] This is clear from St Thérèse's own experiences as given in her autobiographical writings, and from other indications such as the fact that three of her contemporaries left the convent eventually *pour raison grave de santé*, as we are told by Fr François in his notes to his facsimile edition of the *Manuscripts* (Vol II, p. 132). There is a whole library of books on St Thérèse but the magnificent facsimile edition of the original manuscripts of Thérèse's own writings is in a place apart: *Manuscrits Autobiographiques* edited by François de Saint-Marie, OCD (Carmel de Lisieux, 1956). A recent presentation of the saint that can be recommended is *In Search of Thérèse* by Patricia O'Connor (Michael Glazier, Wilmington, Delaware, USA, and Darton, Longman and Todd, London 1987/88).

Passion, especially as imprinted on the Veil of Veronica and on the Shroud of Turin. But as in all aspects of her devotional life, Sr Thérèse saw the devotion as rooted firmly and deeply in Scripture, not only in the synoptic accounts of the Passion, but in the Isaiah description of the Suffering Servant. It is indeed moving to see how Thérèse's own countenance, in successive photographs, takes on something of the image of the crucified, as if her whole being reflected her beloved ever more deeply.

Now if we were to stop at this point we should be left with a portrait of the typical Carmelite sister who manages to reach the basic reality of her calling, having found the reality within and beyond the manifold and extremely subtle unrealities of convent life, with its deadly power-struggles and labyrinthine insincerities, as well as its beauty and holiness and peace. This is indeed a great achievement whether it is arrived at in the cloister or anywhere else, and it has a special clarity and poignancy when it is found in the cloister. It is the heartbeat of Christ in his body which is the Church.

But Thérèse had to face another and deeper challenge, a far more alien and terrifying sifting of reality from illusion, and she had to face this during the period of her physical weariness and dissolution. To grasp the meaning of this, however, it is necessary to see her against the background of her time.

iii. *The Time*
When Sr Thérèse died in Lisieux in late September 1897 in her twenty-fifth year, Pierre Teilhard de Chardin was a tall studious youth of sixteen far away to the south-west, in Clermont-Ferrand, as fascinated by the rocks of his native hills as she had been at the same age by flowers and mosses and the ways of animals and birds: indeed she was almost

as much a scientist by bent and capacity as he was. To the east, a young philosopher named Edmund Husserl was just coming into his power, and his pupils-to-be, Martin Heidegger and Jean-Paul Sartre were serious little boys opening to that human existence which was later to become the burden of their complex and shattering books: Existentialism was lighting the eastern sky, a dawn of strange surrealist tints mingling with the savage red of storms to come, for Adolf Hitler was a brooding boy of ten in an Austrian village. Fifteen years before, two men died whose works lived on for good or ill: Charles Darwin and Karl Marx. The third man of the revolutionary trio that was to dominate the twentieth century was already a professor in Vienna and had already, at forty-three, hit on some of his most disturbing insights: Sigmund Freud had appeared, and he is still with us, at least as a challenge to our powers of self-delusion. Finally, across the English Channel, the great Newman had died eight years before, and Gilbert Keith Chesterton was a lazy and dreamy schoolboy of fifteen, already beginning to feel that the world was 'old and ended' all around him. The phrase is from the dedication poem at the head of his first novel, *The Man Who Was Thursday*, which appeared in 1908, just a decade after Thérèse's death. Addressing an old school friend, Chesterton wrote:

A cloud was on the mind of men and wailing went the weather,
Yea, a sick cloud upon the soul when we were boys together.

A literary critic would not be impressed either by the image or the alliteration, yet this is a haunting couplet, and it does express something of the time into which the *Story of a Soul* began to flow, in 1898. Already Matthew Arnold, who died the year Thérèse entered Carmel, had powerfully expressed this *fin de siècle* mood of total darkness and final

despair in one of the great poems of the nineteenth century,
'Dover Beach':

> The Sea of Faith
> Was once, too, at the full, and round earth's shore
> Lay like the folds of a bright girdle furl'd;
> But now I only hear
> Its melancholy, long, withdrawing roar,
> Retreating to the breath
> Of the night-wind, down the vast edges drear
> And naked shingles of the world.
> . . .
> And we are here as on a darkling plain
> Swept with confused alarms of struggle and flight,
> Where ignorant armies clash by night.

Elizabeth Jennings, who includes this poem in *The
Batsford Book of Religious Verse* (1981), calls it 'a great
poem, a tragic cry which has the poignancy of apparently
unanswered prayer'.

It may be thought that Arnold's poem belongs to a
different world from that of our Carmelite contemplative.
This is true, and it is doubtful whether Thérèse could have
read this poem (in, let us suppose, a good French
translation best made by Arnold himself) with any real
understanding. Any contact she could have made with a
heart bereft of every spark of faith would have been
mediated by her own deep and totally operative faith in the
Divine love and presence. This was entirely true up to the
last eighteen months of her life. Then the whole landscape
of her mind changed, and she would have understood
Arnold's poem completely. Indeed this gentle, cultured,
kindly voice would have provided a relief and release from
the harsh, mocking bitter voices that pressed in on her
from all sides.

Thérèse in these last months experienced to its depths
what Elizabeth Jennings calls 'the poignancy of apparently

unanswered prayer'. Nobody can read her description of this experience as set down in her autobiography without being moved by what she writes, yet she assures us that what she writes is bracketed by reticence, for she feared that a full portrait of her state would shock her little circle of relatives and friends too much. It is here especially that we see the chasm that separated this great cosmic spirit from those around her in her time and place, though we would be quite wrong in reducing them to mere background figures, for every God-given man or woman needs to be recognised by at least a few people in order to become fully part of the human story: this was true even of the Son of God who came down from heaven. But the followers of Jesus did not enter Gethsemane, though they bore witness to it; neither did Thérèse's sisters enter that final darkness though they witnessed it from the outside.

I have tried elsewhere to express something of the existential depth of this experience which put all Thérèse was and believed, all her inner light, totally in question.[2] It is she herself who used a phrase that Heidegger or Sartre might have used thirty years on: *la nuit du néant*, the night of nothingness. I said in that place that it is easy to enter into this darkness as a kind of game or supposition, an 'as if' experience. It is something altogether different to know beyond yea or nay that this is the truth, *la nuit du néant*. To enter this place and inhabit it is to inhabit beforehand the darkest depths of the twentieth century. And it is from this depth that Thérèse spoke and speaks to our time, standing on the threshold of our century.

Some of the men we have recalled brought light and hope to our times in different ways: this is especially true of Teilhard de Chardin and G. K. Chesterton, true also of

---

[2] N. D. O'Donoghue, *Heaven in Ordinarie* (T&T Clark, Edinburgh, 1979) Ch.8.

Newman, true of men from outside the Catholic fold such as Karl Jaspers and Nicolas Berdyaev, true of the great Protestant theologians such as Barth and Brunner. But it would seem that all these men pull back from the gateway of Gethsamene. One can perhaps say that Sartre goes in to the Garden, perhaps Heidegger too, as do many lesser beings, but they do not illuminate the darkness, they do not bring the light with them. By 'light' we do not mean the light of faith, for that is totally obscured, but the light of love, of total self-giving, of final felt and freely accepted annihilation of one's ownmost self. This was what Thérèse did; this is why she shines like a star across the darkest seas of our epoch; this is why the narrow walls of Lisieux Carmel provided a radiance that pierces the scales of our cosmic dragon.

For it is one thing to inhabit the darkness, even the deepest darkness of despair and annihilation; it is another to radiate with a clear steady light from within this darkness. There are two important points here. One is that Thérèse did not simply accept the night of nothingness for her ownmost self; she lived this annihilation day after day, hour after hour, sometimes in the total aloneness of nights of pain, alone with the pain of total unmaking and undoing. The second point is that all through this time she had to support the faith of the whole world as it surrounded her in her enclosed convent, microcosmically and therefore cosmically. It is almost terrifying to see, as one reads her last conversations so carefully preserved by her sisters, how they have unconsciously succeeded in pushing her into the position of being their guide and support. More and more she is the one source of light for them all, ever more profoundly so as she sinks ever more deeply into physical dissolution and total inner darkness.

She held on; she held out. That deepest ground of love

did not give way. Maintain if you like that she was upheld by grace, though this kind of language may be found perfunctory and cheapening. Better to leave the final word about her to herself. 'My vocation is love, to *be love* in the heart of the Church my Mother.' Thus she shines across our century from within the burning heart of the bridal church that is open to all men and women everywhere, for all time.

ST THÉRÈSE OF LISIEUX
IN OUR TIME AND PLACE

i. *The Ministering Angel*
Traditional Catholic piety – that in which St Thérèse grew
up – says that when people die they go to one of three
places or regions or states: heaven, hell or purgatory. There
was, especially in Thérèse's time, a fourth possibility:
limbo, and perhaps we can add this to the eschatological
horizon within which our saint lived and died. Now
Thérèse never questioned this, but as far as she herself was
concerned she quietly put it aside, just as if one looks
closely one finds she quietly put aside the doctrine of
eternal punishment much favoured by the preachers of her
day.

She did not think she was destined for hell or purgatory
or limbo; she was destined for heaven, but in a rather
special sense, a sense in which the traditional conception of
heaven, as a place of rest and a happiness unconcerned with
the woes of earth, was radically transformed. 'I will spend
my heaven,' she said, 'a doing good upon earth.' This was
no pious wish or half-realised commitment: it was at once a
personal and a theological option, deeply felt, constantly
reaffirmed, safely maturing within her even in the dark
days at the end of her life. She did not see this as a specially
high or holy option, and she would freely admit the glory
and greatness of those who longed to be with God and far
away from the vicissitudes of earth. But very definitely and

firmly it was her way and her vocation. The God she knew and loved in the face of Christ Jesus was a God involved in the deepest distresses and miseries, as well as the joys and shafts of glory, of the human condition. Her keen realism would have cut through the tangled rhetoric of some of our 'process' theologians, but she is completely in tune with the deep mystical truth in Process Theology, that God is indeed with man in the days and ways of human history. And, for Thérèse, to be in heaven was to be with God in and with Jesus, the beloved, and to work for the building of the earth. This last phrase is, of course, from Teilhard de Chardin, and it marks the spiritual line of force that unites these two great lovers of God and of the earth.

Those who have opened their lives to this cosmic ministering angel that was and is St Thérèse of Lisieux well know how deep, delicate, continuous and at times unexpected is her presence in one's life. But we are not concerned here with the individual aspect of Thérèse's cosmic presence, but rather with her presence in the Church and in the world, and specifically with three aspects of this presence: Vatican II, feminine theology, and the Carmelite presence in our epoch.

ii. *A New Impulse*
One will not find any mention of St Thérèse of Lisieux in the various historical and doctrinal studies of Vatican II which have appeared over the past twenty-five years and still continue to appear. Yet it is probably safe to say that the one book, apart from the Bible, which had been read and appropriated by practically all the bishops and theologians of the Council was the *Story of a Soul*. Year after year from its first tentative appearance in 1898, the book had spread its influence wider and wider throughout the Catholic world, and its author was first declared

blessed and then canonised within thirty years of her death. She entered every Catholic religious house and seminary, and her 'Little Way' of trust and confidence presented in a new and poignant image the human face of God. Few even among those who were most enthusiastic about her realised the significance of her entry into the night of annihilation, but they all sensed the mighty energy of the spirit that blew out of that cavern of pain and glory in which she died.

Now the Catholic Church in the nineteenth century had become rather fixed and rigid, seeing itself as challenged and attacked by an arrogant secularism and the kind of sophisticated liberalism which lay, in Chesterton's words, 'like a cloud on the minds of men'. This was the age of Pio Nono and the celebrated *Syllabus of Errors* of 1864, which added up to an outright rejection of all that the age stood for under the headings of progress, enlightenment and liberalism. A certain softening of this attitude came with the Pontificate of Leo XIII in 1878, especially in social matters and in the great encyclical *Rerum Novarum* of 1891. The young Thérèse met the aged Pope in 1887, and one can see a parallel between this meeting and that of St Francis with Innocent III seven centuries before. In both cases the Church in the person of its head blessed a new and revolutionary force without in the least realising what was in question.

Again and again in the course of history the free and living flow of the Divine life in the Church becomes sluggish and fixated: concepts rigidify, structures solidify. The really great philosophers and theologians inside and outside the fold view this with alarm and indignation, and a kind of dialectic of traditionalism versus modernism is generated. In a real sense this was the situation into which Jesus came as he faced the conservative Pharisees and the liberal Sadducees. He was crucified by this situation as it was represented by the Sanhedrin, and his blood flowed to make life flow again. This central act and event is enacted again and again in the history of Christendom: a heart impulse, a sacrificial flame, a total self-giving loosens the log jam of ideas and prejudices, frees the hearts of men and women from the catatonic rigidity of conservatism and the heavy grey cloud of liberalism. This is what St Monica did through her son in the fifth century; this is what St Bernard achieved in his time and place; this is what St Ignatius did in the sixteenth century. Above all, this is what St Francis and St Dominic did for the thirteenth century in that explosion of life and that outburst of illumination through the mendicant orders which culminated in Bonaventure and Thomas Aquinas. This is what St Thérèse has given to our time and place: a release of ideas and an enlivening of structures. Her heart-impulse, purified and deepened in the house of reality, opened up to the dimensions of Gethsemane and Calvary in her evening darkness, has become the heart-beat of a Church disencumbered of the weight of a dead past and gradually finding its living future. The fact that we of the older days and the older ways are sometimes disconcerted by it all is not surprising, nor must we cease to affirm boldly that the new ideas and new structures are of no avail unless they allow the mystic and martyred heart of Christendom to beat strongly and lovingly.

iii. *Feminine Theology*
We may begin by distinguishing feminine theology from what is called feminist theology, which has to do with the masculine world of traditional Christian theology. By feminine theology is meant the theology of writers like St Teresa of Avila and St Catherine of Siena inasmuch as it has a certain common quality or tone that distinguishes it from the theology written by men. In our own day we have

feminine theologians such as Simone Weil, Dorothy Sölle and Rosemary Haughton. Rosemary Haughton's *The Passionate God* (Darton, Longman and Todd, London, 1981) aims at being in fact an essay in feminine theology, and is worth reading both on its own merits and as an example of this. One very significant aspect of *The Passionate God* is that it is largely based on the work of the novelist Charles Williams, as the author readily confesses. Williams belonged to the Oxford group that called itself 'The Inklings', which has been elegantly written about in the book of that name by Humphrey Carpenter (Unwin Paperbacks, London, 1981). The most famous members of this group were Williams, C. S. Lewis, and J. R. R. Tolkein. It is clear from this book that there was a side to Williams' character and genius which was almost entirely missing in the other two. Lewis and Tolkein were men at home in a man's world from which women were almost by definition excluded, though both men were devoted in their way to their women folk. Williams was different. He was open to women even more than he was open to men, and his writings show a quality or atmosphere quite missing in the other two, a quality which one may name the feminine. We find the same quality in Paul Tillich when he is compared with the other great theologians of his day, and we find his work widely used by feminine and feminist writers. All sorts of questions arise at this point, but here we are only concerned with giving some kind of sense to the term 'feminine theology' as well as hinting that it is a quality that may be found in men as well as women, though obviously it is in the woman's physical and psychological situation that it finds its primary habitation. It must, nevertheless, be admitted that we are here in a world not yet fully explored or properly defined.

Now St Thérèse is one of the great theologians of
modern times, but she is very definitely a theologian in the
feminine mode. This implies not only deep sensitivity,
vulnerability and openness to the Divine creative fire and
tenderness, but also a deep persuasive irony where true
greatness is apparent littleness, and where what look like
harmless pious clichés are filled with high explosive: thus
dedication to infinite love confers on the dedicated one a
real infinity; to be a living monstrance is to contain the seas
and the stars within one's own body, not metaphorically
but really. (Logical-minded men had trouble with this
during the process of canonisation, as also with Thérèse's
claim that God alone was her guide, a most dangerously
heretical-sounding statement.)

But, of course, the centre of St Thérèse's theology is love
and the primacy of love, a theme that has been very much
exploited since her time by mainstream theology, and that
entered deeply into the whole atmosphere of Vatican II.
But this principle of the primacy of love, as it comes up in
mainstream theology becomes all too easily located in the
head, and only partially accepted by the heart, and
accepted hardly at all as present in the living bodily temple
of flesh and blood. St Thérèse lived this principle not only
in head and heart, not only in body and blood, but in every
cell and every membrane, lived it as a living sacrifice that
consumed her in agony and exhaustion so that in her the
Christ-life might lay hold of human nature at its very
depths. This lived theology she expressed in what she
wrote and what she spoke, using every pious cliché
available to convey it. It is as if she drew all the dying and
dead commonplaces of traditional piety within herself and
brought them forth full of life and truth.

But this power of statement and restatement, this bridal
motherhood of a new Christian age, she did not achieve by

way of the energies available in the oppressively enclosed world of the convent, which was in an exclusive sense a women's world. For this was a place of the feminine absolute just as so many mainstream human centres are dominated by the masculine absolute. In truth however, both the feminine and the masculine are totally relative, relative the one to the other, and when taken as absolutes are destructive of life. Thérèse could be truly creative in a feminine way only by contact with masculine presences. It must be said that the Carmelite structures do in fact leave room for this in the way of spiritual direction; indeed Teresa of Avila insisted on a large freedom in this matter, a freedom, however, easily damaged by despotic superiors and certainly not fully respected in the Lisieux Carmel. It was only by a happy accident that Thérèse managed to meet and talk with the director she desperately needed, the kind of man whose presence, if only once and for a short while, was essential to her.

This was Fr Alexis, a Franciscan through whom the ardent flame of the man of Assisi reached across the centuries to the young woman of that cold time in that cold place, and gave her the seed of freedom, the seed of new life in a new world. She did not see him again. Franciscans, or at least the kind of Franciscan he was, were not much favoured in Lisieux Carmel. But the work had been done in one radiant interview, so separate seeming, for an iron grille divided this man and this woman. It was a meeting of voices in the dark, yet full of life and understanding as such a situation can sometimes be, though it can also block communication. In this case the vital spark that, as Plato says, can alone give philosophical illumination, passed between priest and penitent, however much the priest must have felt the roles were paradoxical. And Thérèse, as she tells us herself, was launched on that special way of total child-like trust that carried her on to Gethsemane and Calvary.

At a certain level this was all she needed, but at a more everyday level she needed more, and a strange and very delicate activity of providence – one can see it as nothing else – intervened to provide this. She was given, in the parlance of her time and place, two missionaries as 'spiritual brothers' from whom she received letters and to whom she wrote at regular intervals. Some of these letters survive, and they are significant and moving, most of all perhaps in their maturing femininity. Obviously this correspondence played an essential role in Thérèse's development as a woman, and as the greatest feminine theologian of our epoch. Especially moving is the little incident a month before her death when she asks her sister to read one such letter that has arrived earlier in the day, but which she had put aside until recreation time. The incident is related to show her self-discipline even in small matters, but it surely reveals first of all a woman opening up beyond the world of the feminine absolute to the world of the creative reciprocity of the feminine and the masculine.

This is not the place to try to set down the main lines of this feminine theology. It has in any case to be felt rather than stated, though its statement in masculine terms by Abbé Combes, Hans Urs von Balthasar and others is legitimate and fruitful. Yet its spirit can only be fully encountered in the text itself, especially in the facsimile edition of Père Francois.[3]

iv. *Carmel Today and Tomorrow*
St Thérèse was and is a gift from God, a light that has descended, like every good gift, from the Father of Lights.

[3] See note ' above.

But a gift is twofold: it must be received as well as given. Indeed it can be said that all human failure is a failure to receive, a failure of response, for God is infinitely good and, as the philosophers say, always in act, always in a great maternal exuberance of giving (to borrow a delicate image from St Francis de Sales). So it is that the story of St Thérèse, and the storm of glory that is the last open chapter of this story, is the story in the first place of a certain family ambience in which this gift from God was nurtured, recognised, cherished and released, into the cloister first and then the cosmos. This family ambience was to remain with this chosen woman right up to her death, but both it and she had been transplanted to the far more testing atmosphere of a Carmelite convent where acceptance became both problematical and painful. It is indeed doubtful if this pure new light would have been seen at all were it not that 'the Martin clan' were there to protect it. For if one examines carefully the character and history of Thérèse's Carmelite companions outside her own sisters and cousin, one sees a dark and broken world that was surely a microcosm of the self-righteous and self-imprisoned Catholicism of the late nineteenth century. Somehow in that time and place this little group of women managed to open their hearts and minds to this light that had come among them.

Outside the enclosure of Lisieux, the wider Carmelite world was waiting and was ready to receive this gift of God with joy and understanding, or at least some sufficient measure of understanding. As time went on it was especially Thérèse's brothers in Carmel who took her into their hearts and minds and presented this cloister gift to Church and Cosmos. There were of course others as well: Franciscans, Jesuits, Dominicans (these especially) and other men and women of every colour and country have given themselves to this gift in response and understanding.[4]

Yet the Carmelite feels a special invitation if not an obligation to receive this gift to the limit of his powers and to communicate it to the wide world. Perhaps one should have said: to receive it to the limit of *her* powers and to communicate it to the limits of *his* powers. But this would be a simplification, for both the more cloistered sister and the less cloistered brother must equally receive the message, live it and understand it. Nor is there any reason why the more cloistered should not become the one who most powerfully communicates the message, should even at times go forth to speak the message. Nor indeed is there any reason why the women should be more cloistered than the men. Here we have the creative tension of cloister and cosmos which is at the centre of the Carmelite principle of praying for the world and teaching the world to pray. This tension does not become creative by making the cloister more cosmic (in the sense of more secular) and asking the cosmos to take on the ways of the cloister. On the contrary, both must be stressed and, to use Hopkins's phrase, *in*stressed. And this especially in the life of the individual Carmelite, who tries to live the life of the cloister in sacrificial love, yet opens the heart and mind to the full dimensions of the human phenomenon in space and time. Within this high and holy commitment there can be times of going forth, times of silence and times of speech, times of cloistered intensity and times of cosmic expansion.

---

[4] Among theologicans the writings of Hans Urs von Balthasar on St Thérèse are especially significant: see the section on 'Saints in the Church' in *The von Balthasar Reader* ed. Kehl and Löser, trans Daly and Lawrence (T&T Clark, Edinburgh, 1982). Among other notable writers who have given attention to Thérèse as a theologian and spiritual guide one may mention: Abbé Combes, Père Philipon, René Laurentin, Guy Gaucher, Jean Guitton, Ronald Knox, Vernon Johnson.

And all times are times of the love of God that is in Christ Jesus, who came by way of Mary Queen Beauty of Carmel, came 'in the spirit and power of Elijah'.

This great matter of the vocation of the Carmelite and the possible reincarnations of the Carmelite principle in the time ahead is too large to pursue any further here. But one point should be made, at least in summary fashion. It is this. We are witnessing in Britain and elsewhere a most disastrous phenomenon: the breakdown of the universities as centres of learning, research and human excellence. More and more the universities are becoming mere factories of professional studies, assembly lines of technicians, doctors, engineers, lawyers, with the odd teacher and clerk as a kind of spin-off. Research is seen more and more in relation to the practical needs of society, of a competitive consumer society. This trend is massive and in, its deepest flow, irreversible. The only hope for humanistic and philosophical studies, the only way to counterbalance this terrifying dehumanisation of the human is for the cloister to resume, in a new way and with a new vision, the task of civilising the cosmos. The Carmelite should be at the heart of this work of enlightenment. One of the most quoted of St Thérèse's sayings is her childhood response when she was asked to choose between various gifts and goodies. 'I take all,' she said. She later saw this as an indication of her whole approach to life and love and all the things of earth and heaven. It is this infinity of mind and heart, this passionate search for true greatness, this vision of total human excellence, that Thérèse shares with her sisters and brothers in Carmel, and with everybody, old and young, Christian and non-Christian, saint and sinner who comes her way. As a ministering angel, just as in her childhood, Thérèse takes all.

CONCLUSION:
HOW DOES IT STAND WITH . . .?

i. *The Carmelite Way*
This book has been concerned with three ardent and
vulnerable individuals, one man and two women, all three
sharing, in very individual ways, a radiance not unmixed
with pathos, yet in its way more powerful than armies in
battle array. One man and two women, all three professed
religious of the Order of Our Blessed Lady of Mount
Carmel, all three dressed in the simple brown habit over
which a white mantle is worn on ceremonial occasions
(thus giving the brethren of the Order the name of White
Friars). This Order is still with us, a constant presence in
the heart of the Church, always renewing itself especially
in its feminine mode, always conscious of its living
continuity with ancient sources.

The Carmelite Order dates from the thirteenth century
when a group of hermits came together at the foot of
Mount Carmel 'near to the Fountain of Elijah' and asked
Albert, the Patriarch of Jerusalem, for a Rule. It was this
'Primitive Rule', as it came to be called, with its careful
balance of contemplation and action, of solitude and
common life, of asceticism and sufficiency, which St Teresa
of Avila and the sixteenth-century Spanish reformers of the
Order reinstated after centuries of adjustment and revision.
Teresa did this with such grace and élan that the principle
of purity never became puritanical, nor the principle of

plainness dead and unimaginative. The world which Teresa shared with John and with her sisters and brothers of the brown habit was, for all its austerity and aspiration, a world of life and laughter, of risk and challenge (the Inquisition was always prowling around), of high adventure and expanding horizons.

Above all, it was a world of men and women, of feminine and masculine, of an *agapé* rooted, sometimes dangerously, in the holy force by which men and women create community and civilisation. If the original impulse was masculine, a group of men receiving a rule from a man, seeing themselves as partaking in the ancient spirit and power of Elijah, yet it looked to the feminine for comfort, companionship and mediation, naming itself as the Order, not of Elijah of Carmel but of the woman from nearby Nazareth who was given the title of the Mountain of Elijah: the Blessed Virgin Mary of Mount Carmel. She is seen as the 'little cloud no larger than a man's hand' that came into view rising from the sea when the prophet prayed for rain on his special holy mountain (1 Kings 18:44). The abundant rain on the parched earth becomes at once the Saviour pierced and flowing on Calvary and also the inundation of light and fire which is *theologia mystica*, the flowing of wisdom and love that liberates and transforms, a liberation theology that is the liberating Word of God in the depths of the heart.[1]

Balancing this original impulse of a masculine open to the feminine is the Teresian impulse, in which the feminine not only sees itself as open to the Most High God but also as deeply and specially concerned with the (masculine)

---

[1] For St John of the Cross and the tradition in which he wrote *Theologia Mystica* was not a theoretical study but an experience of the Divine presence. Perhaps it would be well for us to look again at the ancient understanding of both theology and philosophy as primarily forms of living experience.

priesthood, for St Teresa saw her reformed Carmel as a place of women at prayer for the sanctification of the priesthood. But she also called *men* to share her contemplative vision, and the new Carmel of men arose out of the new Carmel of women. Thus there came about a relationship of equality and companionship that lasts up to our day, and gives the Order a special family feeling which enriches equally both sisters and friars, though some of the latter nurse the illusion that they are the God-given directors of the sisters, not recognising their own need to receive as they give. For neither man nor woman drinks alone of the fountain of mystical prayer and mystical experience. The 'Fountain of Elijah' has its source in that original companionship of man and woman reflecting the countenance of the creator. We must look closely at this source if we are to release this living fountain of Carmelite spirituality into the dark valleys of the future.

ii. *The Marian Mystery*
The Book of Genesis in its essence is the posing of a question, a question that is posed again and again throughout the Old and New Testaments. The question is: How does it stand with humankind? Or at least it is thus the question *seems* to be posed, and it is thus it is posed later on. It is thus it is posed today by all but a minority of commentators on the ways of God and man. A minority has begun to pose it in the form: How does it stand with *woman*kind? This is indeed a legitimate and important question for all of us. But it is not the question which Genesis poses and explores. This question is rather: How does it stand with man and woman?

The answer to, or rather the horizon of this question is that man and woman belong originally together and continue to belong together after undergoing a common catastrophe in their relationship to their source and archetype. For the source of their being is also the image or archetype of the fulness, the clarity and 'nakedness' of their relationship. The light has been dimmed, the glory has been diminished, and as a result their relationship each to each has been changed; no longer is the one a clear and radiant mirror of the other, in the joy of belonging and the joy of bringing forth. A shadow of *having* has fallen across the clear and holy mirror of their *being*. In their darkened world 'he/she that is' mingles with, or is invaded by, 'that which holds and has'. Man and woman have set out on a long road of mutual disharmony, exploitation and destructiveness.

But the light has not been extinguished, nor has the glory entirely departed. This is clear from the subsequent history of man and woman, from the emergence of Abel, from the fact that men began to call on the name of the Lord (Genesis 4:26), and paradoxically from the story of the Flood by which ancient purity is re-established and the image of God in man is reaffirmed (Genesis 9:6).

When Elijah the Tishbite suddenly appears on the scene (1 Kings 17:1–16) the question: How does it stand with humankind? receives an ambiguous answer (1 Kings 18:21), and Elijah challenges this ambiguity and slays the priests of Baal (*Ibid.* 18:40). We are not concerned here with the uniquely dramatic story of these happenings (1 Kings 17–19) but with the light which this story provides as we ask: How stands it with man and woman? At first sight Elijah comes as a man in a man's world, yet if we look more closely we see that the whole story of Elijah is the story of the prophet's relationship to two women. There is the widow of Zarephath who sustains him, not only by her ministrations but by her total faith in his prophetic word (1 Kings 17:13–16). She is nameless, yet her presence is vivid and entirely significant, so much so that she appears again in St Luke's Gospel in one of the few references made by Jesus to incidents from the Old Testament (Luke 4:26) and more importantly in the story of the widow of Nain (Luke 7:11). On the other side there is Jezebel, the woman who worships Baal and stands firm by her own understanding of life right up to her terrible death. She is so powerfully possessed by her deity or demon that in the moment of his triumph Elijah fears her and runs away (1 Kings 19:3), and her image survives to trouble the man who kills her so cruelly and self-righteously (2 Kings 9:34).[2]

What can reach us today from this ancient source? What has the presence of Elijah to say to the men and women who accept the ancient prophet as their preceptor and father? Or, rather, what is there for us today and in the days ahead in this tradition that has its source in the mystic vision of Genesis and pulses through the dramatic story of Elijah and the two women, the woman who protected him and the other who sought to kill him?

Already here at the source itself, in the relationship of the prophet-man with the women who stand with him and against him, there is ambiguity. Yet the Carmelite tradition as it emerges in the thirteenth century has healed this ambiguity by a stroke of mystical genius which places the feminine at the very heart of the life of contemplation by

---

[2] A remarkable novel, *Jezebel and the Dayspring*, by Flavia Anderson, a professed Christian, tries to tell this archetypal story (which surfaces again in the confrontation of Herodias and John the Baptist) from the woman's point of view (Chapman and Hall, London, 1949). In a modern instance of this archetypal confrontation, that of John Knox and Mary, Queen of Scots, both sides of the story are told, yet from the Knox standpoint Mary was no better (indeed no other) than Jezebel. It seems to me that the Scottish conscience (Protestant and Catholic) is still struggling with this conflict, not as historical 'unfinished business' but as a decision to accept or reject its own feminine and/or its own masculine side.

dedicating (for the first time in Christian history) the whole enterprise to the Woman of Nazareth seen as the Queen Beauty of Carmel: *Regina, Decor Carmeli*. In other words the original source from which flows the Fountain of Elijah is affirmed in all its freshness and innocence in the image and 'imagination' (in Blake's sense) of a woman who is not only queen but also sheds all around that rugged mountain the sacrament of human beauty.

We do not know how consciously these thirteenth-century ascetics opened their hearts to this beauty of womanhood as a mediation of God's grace and beauty. All we do know is that they placed the celestial-feminine at the very centre of their contemplative vision, seeing themselves as the 'hermits of Our Blessed Lady of Mount Carmel'. This dedication can have the sound of a pious cliché that rolls easily off the tongue and says no more than that these men reduced the feminine to a controllable fantasy, a woman 'cleansed' of all the pain and passion and pathos – and holiness – of living women. But this would be unfair as a generalisation; it would overlook certain experiences of deep anguish, of breakdown and breakthrough, of that panic and despair which the true follower of the Man of Gethsemane and Calvary have to *face* (and not merely encounter and evade), experiences by which a man learns his original and total dependence on the feminine, in which he does indeed explore his own *anima* but also comes to realise that it is not good for him to be alone, or rather that a dark pit of eternal loneliness opens out at his feet. Here, like Isaiah, he calls on the living God (Isaiah 40:26); here with his Master he calls on the Father (Matthew 26:39), but if he is true to the fulness of the experience it is only the Mother-Face of God, the Mother-Presence of the Father that will support him, though the final source of this is that whose image is man and woman together.

The Virgin Mary of the Christian mystic, truly such, is not a controllable fantasy-woman, rather does she meet him in the deepest dungeon of unmaking and annihilation carrying the child in her arms who is life in the pit of death: without the woman the child is not there. So it is that in the Celtic (thoroughly mystical) tradition Jesus is always 'the Son of Mary'.[3] So it is that for the mystic (at least the *Carmelite* mystic) the words of Jesus about the absolute necessity of becoming a child to enter the Kingdom of heaven is seen as involving a very concrete experience of child-mother relationship. There may be other mysticisms which can ignore the feminine, though one may doubt it. But in Carmelite mysticism the Virgin Mary is essential, central, all-pervasive: *totus Carmelus est Marianus*.[4] And it is true equally of both branches of the Carmelite family, for not all Carmelites even in Spain accepted the Teresian reform (which came to be called the Order of *Discalced* Carmelites), and there were other reforms before and since of what came to be called the Order of Calced Carmelites or Carmelites of the Ancient Observance. The link with Elijah is accepted by both branches of the Order but it is the pervasiveness and richness of the Marian-Feminine presence that is, above all, the signature of Carmel.

In Teresa and Thérèse, as in the women of Carmel in general, the Marian presence takes the form of a sympathetic identification which finds its grounds in the first two chapters of St Luke, especially the Magnificat, and also in the accounts of the Passion in all four evangelists. Mary is presented by St Luke as meditating the Christ-mystery

[3] See A. Carmichael, *Carmina Gadelica*, five volumes (Scottish Academic Press, Edinburgh, 1900–1934), *passim*.

[4] Literally: 'The totality of Carmel is Marian'. The usual English version runs: 'Without Mary Carmel is nothing'. This does not say that the *Christian* depends totally on Mary, but that the *Carmelite* way of being a Christian loses its specific quality if the Marian presence is not accepted.

contemplatively (Luke 2:16, 51), and the Carmelite-feminine renews this meditation in every time and place.[5] The Carmelite 'idea' sees this human response and 'cradling' of Christ as essential to the ongoing on-flowing incarnation. The Eucharist is central to this: the Carmelite-feminine mothers the ever-descending Word through this total dedication and immolation. Whoever comes to the door of a Carmelite convent comes to meet something of the mystery of the Word made flesh. Sr Elizabeth of the Trinity offered herself as 'another humanity in which Christ renews his mysteries'.[6] This is not womanhood unfulfilled but woman totally fulfilled as cloister and cosmos become one.

But this fulfilment needs a certain mediation through the presence of manhood, and we find this amply exemplified in the case of St Teresa who was a very feminine woman most of all in her openness to the masculine. Unfortunately our language is very poor in the vocabulary of the kind of mystical relationship which is at once full of tenderness and

[5] Twice in the course of the Infancy Narrative St Luke shows us Mary in a contemplative posture. In the midst of the story of the shepherds and 'the heavenly host' we are told that 'Mary kept all these things pondering them in her heart' (RSV); again at the end of the Temple story that concludes the infancy narrative we find that Mary 'kept all these things in her heart'. This twice-repeated presentation of the feminine-contemplative is itself remarkable enough in that it breaks in on the story-line in each case and in that essentially the same formula is repeated. It is even more remarkable in the vivid immediacy of the terms used in the Greek original: the verb *terein* which occurs in both v.19 and v.51 is better translated 'to treasure' as in the NEB version: with the prepositions *syn* and *dia* it becomes stronger and more active. The word for 'pondering' in v.19 is *synballousa* and is also strong and vivid. All in all it seems clear that, for St Luke, Mary provides the necessary ground of consciousness into which 'the things which have been spoken' (the *rhēmata*) are received.

[6] *Elizabeth de la Trinité, Oeuvres Completes* (Editions du Cerf, Paris, 1979) T.II, p. 126, the original reads: *'Esprit d'amour, survenez en moi, afin qu'il se passe en mon âme comme une incarnation du verbe; que je lui sois un humanité de surcroit en laquelle Il renouvelle son mystère'.* An editorial note points out that the key phrases here came through two priests, Fr. Fages and Mgr. Gay. This kind of co-operation is typical of the life of Carmel.

understanding yet for all that free of self-indulgence and possessiveness; which has its ups and downs, its 'history', its ironies, its conflicts, its pedagogy as each learns to accept the other, for man and woman are eternally and gloriously 'out of step' yet capable of walking hand in hand into the deepest mysteries of life, death and resurrection. Certainly St Teresa's main 'soul-friendship', that with Fr Gracian, cost her dear in terms of misunderstanding and heartbreak, yet it was he most of all who was the begetter of her books and foundations; he, on his part, had a price to pay after Teresa's death when he became the target of Doria and the 'Regularisers', and was finally deprived of the Carmelite habit, ending his days with the Brethren of the Ancient Observance.

There is a sense in which Gracian rather than John was the *man* of the Carmelite reform: at least so St Teresa saw him. John was indeed a mystical and poetic genius, the culminating point of Dionysian mysticism in the West, and here Gracian cannot be compared with him. Gracian's energy and flexible charm is in striking comparison with John's quiet reserve and unbreakable integrity. Yet both men were equally open to the feminine and were indeed under a common accusation by their more earth-bound brethren of being gravely at fault in their relationships with the sisters. Here, most deeply perhaps, the signature of Carmel became the sign of the Cross not only for Gracian and John but for the women whose love of them and from them was put so cruelly in question.[7]

---

[7] An account of the events touched on here will be found in any of the more complete lives of St John of the Cross (Crisogono, Bruno, Ruiz, Allison Peers), as also in Silverio's history of the Carmelite Reform. It is from the perspective of mystical relationships, especially, that John's insistence on asceticism can be understood. Without this continuing asceticism all mystical love becomes self-indulgent and destructive.

One would not want to linger over this point, not only because the language we have to use – late twentieth-century English – is incapable of dealing with mystical friendship in any detail, but also because the main point is sufficiently clear: that the Carmelite Reform of the sixteenth century was not monosexual (as seems to have been the case with other Orders and reforms) but a living dialogue between men and women, with all the vicissitudes, perils, misunderstandings and vitality that this implies. St Teresa placed herself and her sisters behind a grille, not because she wanted a world without men but precisely to stabilise this dialogue and allow its harmonies to grow and flourish. In the cold 'neutered' atmosphere of Northern Europe the barrier was kept and its positive purpose overlooked.

In this world of man-woman dialogue and dialectic the Humanity of Jesus Christ and the Humanity of Mary, the 'Woman' of the Johannine Scriptures (John 2:4; 19:26; Revelation 12) is of far more than devotional importance. It makes the central and centering statement about man and woman. This statement belongs not to the realm of evasive fantasy but to the realm of mystical imagination, that is to say, it is an expression of a shared source-experience of shattering and transforming presence and power: the love of God in the heart of God's image, at once male and female. In a devotional tradition parallel to the Carmelite this became the presence of the *hearts* of Jesus and Mary, the one thorn-crowned, the other pierced to the centre, both glowing and radiant. This other tradition has lent itself too easily to sentimentality and a soggy, evasive spirituality. In its truth, however, it is full of spiritual power and human aspiration. It expresses better than any other symbol the pathos and poignancy, the mutual love and fealty, the ultimate and eternal glory of manwomanhood, the countenance of the Most High in Mary the bridal-mother and in Jesus at once son and bridegroom, at once divine and human. It expresses that same countenance reflected in human history in holy men and women, that is to say, in all men and women who open fully to their destiny and destination.[8]

Carmelite spirituality speaks of the Humanity of Christ rather than the Heart of Christ, but in the one case as in the other the symbol is more than a symbol. It is also a reality at its own level of the inner or spiritual body. It is this reality that St Teresa was fighting for in the texts presented in Chapter 4. In the case of the Woman, Carmelite devotion sees her as a kindling and glowing presence, again not a mere fantasy to meet a certain mood but an image expressing a depth-experience at once total and continuous: the very life and breath of Carmel. Without this living feminine presence, known and felt, renewing itself each day with morning freshness (the *stella matutina*) and evening quietness (the *stella vespertina*), at once mother of the world's grief (*mater dolorosa*) and fountain of hope and joy (*causa nostrae laetitiae*) even where all seems broken, dark and destructive (*refugium peccatorum*); – without this presence of the Woman there is nothing special or worth preserving in the Order of the Blessed Virgin Mary of Mount Carmel. Everything else is found better elsewhere.

This presence of Mary expresses itself very concretely in what is called the Brown Scapular, a band of cloth worn over the shoulders which is seen as a living contact with the Woman clothed with the sun and a shield against the powers of darkness. The Carmelite Scapular can become a

---

[8] On the Bridegroom-Bride relationship of Christ (as the second or true Adam) and Mary (as the second or true Eve) see Otto Semmelroth, *Mary, Archetype of the Church*, tr. by von Erdes and Devlin, with an introduction by Jaroslav Pelikan, (Gill and Son, Dublin, 1963).

talisman and an evasion, but in its truth it is rather the feminine aspect of the armour of God set down in masculine terms by St Paul (Ephesians 6). To accept 'the livery of Mary' is to enter more deeply into the spiritual combat with all its vulnerability and paradoxes, for in this conflict power is made perfect in infirmity (2 Corinthians 12:9).

In the traditional ikon of the Scapular (associated with the English Carmelite, St Simon Stock) the Virgin-Mother is represented with the Child Jesus in her arms, so that the Scapular is given by the child rather than by the Mother, yet both child and gift are carried by the Woman, in a real sense earthed by the Woman. There is no way of understanding this co-operation of mother and child, of feminine and masculine, if we limit ourselves to a logic of exclusion and a discourse of exclusion, as if what is affirmed of the one were negated of the other. The ancient and continuing discourse of Carmelite spirituality insists, or rather assumes, that the more greatly Mary is honoured and invoked the more greatly Christ Jesus is honoured and invoked. Here the distinction between totality and infinity, on which Emmanuel Levinas grounds his whole philo-sophy, is helpful.[9] There is not a totality within which Christ and Mary have to be placed over against each other, but rather an infinity in which one horizon calls forth another. The Marian horizon opens out to the infinity of the Divine Logos, yet the Divine Logos is always the incarnate Logos born of the Woman and opening up the mystery of the Mother-countenance of God. The moment we try to transpose this discourse into the discourse of totality-logic we are back to all the debates concerning the 'place' of Mary and the 'place' of the feminine in God's

---

[9] *Totalité et Infini* (Martinus Nijhoff, La Haye, 1971).

self-revelation. These debates have their place in the world
of system and systematisation, and this world must be
respected. But they must not enclose mystical aspiration
nor imprison mystical imagination.

iii. Feminism and After

There is a useful scholastic distinction between *actus
exercitus* and *actus signatus*. What happens in the order of
'exercise' is as it were blind, like the little man in Molière's
comedy who was speaking prose all his life unknown to
himself. It is in this way that the Carmelite spiritual
tradition has been deeply and continuously exploring and
developing, painfully and joyfully, 'in sickness and in
health' the feminine and masculine in living relationship to
their source in the Most High God who created manwomanhood in His own image. Yet this phenomenon has
not by any means emerged into the order of 'signification',
as something grasped, recognised, expressed, or communi-
cated. If it is true that the mystical is in one of its primitive
meanings that which is hidden or esoteric, that which must
not be taken outside the sanctuary or *fanum* to the profane
world, then it may be said that this situation was in a sense
deliberate. For the spiritual when it manifests itself to
unspiritual eyes and ears is at once misapprehended. It is at
best not understood and at worst misunderstood according
to the common dialectic of misunderstanding by which
events and actions are seen as their opposites. Thus the
holiness of Jesus was seen as blasphemy and his saving
presence as destructive. Every true mystic knows this and
so he or she is silent unless the law of charity calls for plain
speaking.

   In our time a phenomenon is arising which is of
incalculable consequences. It is the awakening of woman-
kind to the rights of woman as the revolutionaries of two

centuries ago awakened to the rights of man. In effect these men were posing the question: How does it stand with humankind? But it was a question heavily weighted on the side of the masculine: the voices raised on behalf of the rights of woman were few and isolated, and easily dismissed as irrelevant. In our day this has begun to change very rapidly. Now the question: How does it stand with woman? is asked on every side, is asked especially in the New World with all the energy and freshness (still remaining) of a people come of age.

This question had to be asked, and the asking of it worldwide marks a radical change in human consciousness. Yet in itself it is a divisive and destructive question, a question usually based on the false assumption that there is an absolute feminine as in the past (and up to now) so much conflict and destruction has come from the absolute masculine, men refusing to grow into that maturity of manhood in which a man's whole being finds its deepest meaning in living relationship with the feminine. It may be argued that the absolute feminine must 'even up' by affirming its rights over against the masculine, but this would be simply an imitation of what has already proved divisive and destructive, a re-affirmation of our neutered world and our neutered churches. For it is by no means a man's world in the sense of a world of truly masculine men. Rather is it a neutered world in which men have failed to know what it is to be fully masculine.

It is not man as masculine that fails to take full account of the feminine, for the taking of full account of the feminine is the definition of man as masculine. It is rather the neutered man of the absolutised masculine that is guilty of this betrayal of the Divine image. And this betrayal is being compounded by the emergence of the absolute feminine.

Feminism in some of its forms – by no means in all of its forms – asks the wrong question. The question that has to be asked is not: How does it stand with woman? But: How does it stand with man and woman?[10] Another way of posing the question is: How goes it with the making of the world? For it is a terrible mistake to think that the world has been made by some invulnerable and uninvolved deity – Sartre's *Dieu Fabricateur* – far off and inaccessible. This is the hard Satanic theology of the hard Satanic God of religious fundamentalism. The God who is at the source of the mystical fountains, the God of Elijah and the Carmelite tradition, is a Spirit ever awakening within the hearts of men and women, ever discovering anew *and afresh* her/his own image in the dialogue of masculine and feminine. From this theological perspective the answer to the question: How does it stand with the making of the world? finds its full meaning and can open out towards its proper horizon, for only thus can such a question find an answer.

This question in the context of what has been outlined reveals a new horizon of the world's making, reveals in a sense a world unmade, yet a world in the making. As man looks in awe and terror over the rim of the third Christian millenium he knows that no hope lies in the world he has made, the world made through him. He is forced to seek once again, as at the beginning, the companionship of the woman and to realise that all he has been working at is but the projection of his own isolated heart and mind. There is

[10] In what is perhaps the most important feminist book on Christian origins Elizabeth Schussler Fiorenza expresses her aim as follows: 'I simply mean to raise the question: How can early Christian origins be reconstructed in such a way as to be understood as "women's affairs?" In other words, is early Christian history "our own" history or heritage? Were women as well as men the initiators of the Christian movement?' *In Memory of Her* (SCM Press, London, 1983) p. xviii. The first two questions are simply an expression of neutered thinking, valid only as 'balancing the books' within a neutered world. The third question escapes from this way of thinking, but only if we substitute 'with' for 'as well as'.

no help to be had from the kind of woman who has become masculinised by the world of man's politics and projects, nor yet from the woman who has domesticated man for her own security. He is looking for the mystical woman as she is looking for the mystical man. And everything written above is simply an effort to delineate this man and this woman as a possibility at least partly realised in the ancient crucible of Carmel.

Perhaps the word 'delineate' is too strong. The Carmelite experience, in its success and failure, in its confusions and contradictions, in its turmoil and aspiration is but the first tentative sketch of a new world in which the companionship of men and women goes beyond both the biological and the familial, recovers however painfully something of that first Christian élan of virginity and celibacy that only survived as long as the glow of the Master maintained its original freshness. Yet this élan is still with us, is still available to us as it was to St Paul when he said 'I live now, not I but Christ lives in me' (Galatians 2:20). This is no metaphorical statement, but the affirmation of a reality far more powerful in its impact than wind and weather, than the physical blood in vein and artery. The Fourth Gospel speaks of the branch and the vine to express this élan, this flow of life, and the image affirms both the need for total openness to this source of life and also the need for the branch *to be itself* in every least particle and cell of its structure: grace must *respect* nature. The Christian call to holiness must respect the nature of man and the nature of woman and the *total* relativity of feminine and masculine. Only thus can we begin to give a Christian answer to the question: How does it stand with man and woman?

INDEX